CREATING YOUNG MARTYRS

CREATING YOUNG MARTYRS

Conditions that Make Dying in a Terrorist Attack Seem Like a Good Idea

Alice LoCicero and Samuel J. Sinclair

Contemporary Psychology
Chris E. Stout, Series Editor

PRAEGER SECURITY INTERNATIONAL
Westport, Connecticut · London

Library of Congress Cataloging-in-Publication Data

LoCicero, Alice, 1945–
   Creating young martyrs : conditions that make dying in a terrorist attack seem like a good idea /
   Alice LoCicero and Samuel J. Sinclair.
      p. cm. — (Contemporary psychology, ISSN 1546–668X)
   Includes bibliographical references and index.
   ISBN-13: 978–0–275–99690–1 (alk. paper)
1. Child terrorists. 2. Child suicide bombers. 3. Terrorists. 4. Terrorism. I. Sinclair, Samuel J.,
1975– II. Title.
HV6431.L63 2008
363.325'11—dc22   2008020459

British Library Cataloguing in Publication Data is available.

Library of Congress Catalog Card Number: 2008020459
ISBN-13: 978–0–275–99690–1
ISSN: 1546–668X

First published in 2008

Praeger Security International, 88 Post Road West, Westport, CT 06881
An imprint of Greenwood Publishing Group, Inc.
www.praeger.com

Printed in the United States of America

The paper used in this book complies with the
Permanent Paper Standard issued by the National
Information Standards Organization (Z39.48–1984).

10 9 8 7 6 5 4 3 2 1

To All Who Work for a World Free of Terror

Alice LoCicero:
To Emily Dawn and James Alexander. My love for you has inspired me to work for a better world for all future generations. And to my Dearest Dennis, who supports even my outlandish plans.
And to my friend, colleague, and mentee, Samuel J. Sinclair, who challenged me to accomplish things that were, in theory, impossible.

Samuel J. Sinclair:
To my love, Tate, and my two freight trains, Cole and Reese—my three treasures who give me the ultimate reason and meaning to do what it is I do.
I also dedicate this book to my friend, colleague, and mentor, Alice LoCicero, who on a fall 2002 day gave me a chance when no one else would and let it fly.

The representation of some individuals described, quoted, or interviewed for this book has been altered to protect their identities.

CONTENTS

Preface   ix

Acknowledgments   xvii

CHAPTER 1: Growing Up in War Zones: Children and the   1
        Communities that Love Them

CHAPTER 2: The Social Science of Terrorism   9

CHAPTER 3: Cognitive Development: The Brilliant, Exasperating,   31
        Deliberate Adolescent Mind

CHAPTER 4: When Will the War End? "Never."   51

CHAPTER 5: Most Victims of War Are Civilians   71

CHAPTER 6: The Invisible Global Network: Envisioning a   91
        Nonviolent Path to Peace

Notes   111

References   115

Index   119

About the Series   123

About the Authors   127

PREFACE

Alice LoCicero's Thoughts

Steps in the development of this project seem best described as snapshots—vivid memories of points in time. I include three of many memories here.

Memory One: September 13, 2001, 1 pm, Social Psychology Class

Professors catch bits of conversation as students enter class, hoping some of the conversation can be woven into the lecture. On this day, there was plenty to catch, and as the professor, I realized that the students' experiences of the last forty-eight hours were both germane to the subject, and more than worthy of class time. I asked students to share their comments and questions with the entire class. There was a lot going on.

My roommate went home.
A lot of people went home.
I could not watch.
I was glued to the TV.
How could they do that?
What is going to happen to the people in New York now?
What religion tells you to murder thousands of people?
Did you know anyone?
What sort of person would kill himself in order to kill a lot of other people?
Do all Muslims believe this? All Arabs?
How did they plan it? Did their families know?
Why didn't someone stop them?

Social Psychology is full of surprises. Students find out that many of the things they took for granted about themselves and others are false. Ingenious researchers have shown that there are fascinating patterns about the way we interact. But a diverse group of students in a Social Psychology class in an urban university had barely begun to study these social psychology classics when more immediate concerns, also germane to social psychology, grabbed their attention. Two days earlier, several men had boarded planes in an airport less than five miles from campus and blown up the World Trade Center in New York, killing thousands, and scaring the citizens of the world. The students wanted to know what psychology had to offer by way of explanation. The questions students asked reflect a list of key puzzles that the United States would have to solve in the coming years. Nearly seven years later, their list still holds. We have progressed on some, but there is still a lot of thinking and learning to do. Here are the key questions the students asked:

1. How shall we comfort those close to us who have lost friends and family?
2. How shall we cope with our own fears and shock?
3. Why would someone do this?
4. Did the terrorists' families know? Why didn't they stop them?
5. How can so many people see Osama bin Laden as a hero?
6. How could religion possibly justify mass murder?
7. What is the role of suicide in terrorism?
8. Will it happen again?
9. Why Boston? Why New York? Why the United States?
10. Things are not normal now. Will they ever get back to normal?
11. How will we protect our Muslim friends?
12. Why are so many people already attacking innocent Arabs and Muslims in the United States?
13. Can history and psychology help us understand this event?
14. Is Boston safe?
15. How can the United Nations and other international organizations see to it that these things stop happening?

The very freedom to ask these questions and try to answer them in an open and objective manner is the central gift of living in a democracy with a functional legal infrastructure and a constitution that protects the right of free speech. At the same time, the lack of knowledge of cultures, of religions, of the experience of living with terror, disappearances, mass murder with impunity, and secret torture that seemed like a luxury a week earlier had become the curse of ignorance that accompanied the blessing of relative safety and personal empowerment that Americans enjoyed.

In the process of beginning to answer these questions, then, Americans learned that the events of 9/11, though central and critical to us, were little more than a blip in the record of mass murder of civilians in recent decades. Terrorism—whether sponsored by the state in such eras as Hitler's Germany, Maoist China, or Stalinist Russia, or by nonstate-sponsored groups such as the Shining Path in Peru, or the Lord's Resistance Army in Uganda—has been alive and active as a method for centuries—perhaps millennia—and it exists in many parts of the world today. If we are to understand 9/11, then, we have to think harder, work longer, and look more closely at historical and contemporary world events—something most Americans thought we had the luxury of more or less ignoring. We now know that we do not live in a safe bubble, and we must reassess our place in the global community.

Memory Two: September 6, 2002, 11 am, Meeting with Samuel J. Sinclair

One year after the 9/11 attacks, I had expected that the public would have a full understanding of terrorism, terrorist leaders, their followers and supporters. I had thought that all the questions asked by my students a year earlier could be answered. I was beginning to get impatient, and to ask what I could contribute to the effort to understand, when Samuel Sinclair, a new doctoral student met with me, hoping I would be his research advisor.

Two weeks into graduate school, he was ready to lay out his research agenda for the next five years: He, like the students in the Social Psychology class, wanted to know everything there was to know about terrorism, its leaders, their followers, and their victims. Thus, we embarked on a set of joint projects that included studies of Osama bin Laden, of the impact of terrorism and fear of future terrorism, of various theoretical approaches to terrorism, and of children who intentionally die in a terrorist action. Along the way, we established the Society for Terrorism Research.

This book sets out to contribute to ongoing scientific efforts to answer some of the questions that, nearly seven years after the 9/11 attacks, are still unanswered. We believed it was important to know how children become involved in terrorist groups, and how it happens that they engage in attacks in which they intentionally die.

Memory Three: May 24, 2007, Bandaranaike Airport, Colombo, Sri Lanka

Researching the conditions that favor children becoming terrorists, we found, required actual immersion in at least one of the areas where it is common. No

one had published answers to the questions we wanted to ask, and few psychologists had actually visited places where there was ongoing conflict. It had taken nearly a year of persistent efforts—following up every possible lead—but a trip was arranged, and our research had received approval from the Institutional Review Board at the university. After nearly thirty hours of travel, I arrived in Sri Lanka, and a representative of a small nonprofit organization that had helped me make the trip was here to greet me. I had three weeks to learn all I could. Fortunately, the people of Sri Lanka lived up to their reputation for being kind and generous, the translators were skilled and generously shared their knowledge of the culture, and many children and adults spoke to me freely, after being promised complete anonymity. Many of my questions were answered. Like all good research, however, many new ones arose. This book would have been impossible without the help of my hosts, translators, and all the children and adults who answered my many questions. To protect their anonymity, I kept no information that would identify the people who answered my questions. In order to get the research data back to the United States safely, in this Internet age, I e-mailed it all, password protected, from wherever I could find a connection.

Perhaps predictably, I came to love the island and the people, and began planning my return trip, hopefully in late 2008 or early 2009, even before I left.

Samuel J. Sinclair's Thoughts

As of writing these words, it has been roughly six years since the terrorist attacks of 9/11. I was working in a downtown Boston skyscraper when my wife called to tell me that a small plane had crashed into one of the World Trade Center towers in New York City. As I spoke to her, the second plane crashed into the World Trade Center tower. As she said this, I knew we were under attack and remember thinking that life as I knew it had changed. As the reports came out that the planes had originated in Boston, it crossed my mind that we should get out of our building. I would probably have to help my supervisor down the stairs on my shoulders in the event something happened, given her physical limitations, so began coming up with an evacuation plan. As I thought about what to do, a third plane hit the Pentagon. This was like War of the Worlds.

Several days later, I was riding my bike home from work through Copley Square to find the police had shut down several square blocks. Thousands of people were amassed outside of one popular hotel, along with a police presence I had never seen before. The reports coming out of the crowds were that some of the 9/11 terrorists' handlers were holed up in the hotel waiting for Air Traffic Control to allow planes into the air so they could leave the country. The next day I called the Marine Corps recruiter near me, and asked to join. After several meetings with them, they advised me not to join and to continue my life the way it was. They told me that my reasoning had too much to do with seeking

vengeance, and not enough with becoming a Marine. They also argued that they had more than enough soldiers to fight this war, and there would likely be little to no ground troops when it came time to respond. Our response would rather be an annihilation of the enemy using precision-guided weapons and waves of bombers. Thus, there was no urgent need to recruit at that moment. I found this somewhat ironic later, given how stretched our military has now become in multiple theaters of war.

About a month later came the anthrax attacks, which only reinforced my belief that we as a country were under attack. At the time, I was reading anything I could get my hands on, both published works and material on the Internet, to better understand what was happening, who these people were, and why they were attacking our country. I was voracious in my consumption of anything terrorism-related. I needed to know everything I could to understand this threat. From a psychological point of view, I was hyperaroused and could not focus on anything else, work or otherwise. Everyone around me had begun returning to normal lives, and the threat of terrorism seemed to fade as time passed. This was until 2002, when the Department of Homeland Security instituted the color-coded alert system, and began issuing "credible threats" to the public and raising the threat level to Orange: High Risk of Attacks. Then came the Bali attacks in 2002, the Madrid attacks in 2004, the London attacks in 2005, and the various smaller-scale attacks in multiple other countries including Saudi Arabia, Morocco, Indonesia, and Chechnya.

Over the course of my scholarship on terrorism, several things really surprised me. First, there had been little in the academic and scientific communities (social science or otherwise) that has existed on terrorism, particularly as it relates to this new strand of terrorism rooted in extreme Islamic ideology—as opposed to the more secular, political terrorists of the 1970s. I was struck at how much we lacked an understanding of both the psychology of terrorists and the psychological impact of terrorism in general, and how there are myriads of "experts" espousing myriads of theories, which are often contradictory, about these issues.

The second thing that surprised me was how much the world has changed in terms of how we as a society move forward. We now live in a world of color-coded terrorism alert systems and "credible threats." An example of this phenomenon is when the Department of Homeland Security and former Massachusetts Governor Mitt Romney warned the city of Boston a few years ago (in 2004) that several Chinese nationals had crossed the border from Mexico into Southern California and were on their way to Boston to detonate a nuclear device. People were randomly searched on the commuter trains coming into the city, and people expressed their fears, frustrations, and anxieties on multiple news interviews broadcast to the region. As has been the case since 9/11, these threats eventually turned out to be false. Regardless, however, these threats affect people.

A final comment on why we think a deeper understanding of terrorism and terrorist motivations are relevant and necessary. In addition to the fact that there had not been a lot written about modern terrorism, rooted in radical interpretations of Islam as opposed to the politically motivated terrorism of the 1970s, much of what has been communicated has been suspect at best. For example, arguing that terrorists hate us for our values and freedoms is just simply nonproductive, as it boils down a very complex set of issues into an oversimplified formula: terrorist attacks occur because terrorists hate our freedom. Common sense tells you there is much more to it than this. Common sense also tells you that this is a dangerous road to go down, as it fundamentally misconstrues the issues and subsequent response.

In the books and articles that were written on the topic post–9/11, there have been several outstanding analyses on this issue. Recently, the former head of the Bin Laden unit at CIA, Michael Scheuer, left the agency and published several books (including *Imperial Hubris*) on the current terrorist threat using public source material. Among many things, Scheuer argues that bin Laden himself has been the most accurate predictor/reporter of attacks that follow in his frequent public statements. That is to say, when bin Laden has said in the past that he plans to attack he follows through. Interestingly, immediately following 9/11, Scheuer also reports that bin Laden was heavily criticized in the Islamic community for: (1) not acquiring religious approval for the attacks; and (2) not properly warning the United States and allowing its citizens to accept Allah prior to carrying out the operations. As if to address this proactively for the next set of attacks, Scheuer reports that bin Laden sought and acquired religious approval from a Saudi Arabian cleric in 2004 to kill four million Americans, the amount that has been estimated by bin Laden to have been killed by western troops operating on the Arabian peninsula since 1991.

As Scheuer has suggested, we should consider what bin Laden himself is saying about the future. In his recent audiotape of January 16, 2006, bin Laden (BBC News translation) says, "As for the delay in carrying out similar operations in America, this was not due to failure to breach your security measures. Operations are under preparation, and you will see them on your own ground once they are finished, God willing." This was part of the same tape where he offered the United States a truce, if we pulled out of the Arabian peninsula. The bottom line is that we do not understand terrorism or terrorists well, and what has been done is incomplete. This book is an attempt to contribute to an area of research that is not well understood, and is driven by our own fear of what is to come.

Why is this research so important? In short, it is because we believe terrorism is the most significant threat to the peace of the world, and will continue to be so for the foreseeable future. We believe that our children will be dealing with this threat when they are our ages. We do not believe the terrorist threat has abated, and we do believe more is to come. We also believe that what will follow will

be extreme. In his book, *Nuclear Terrorism,* Harvard University Dean and Professor, Graham Allison, estimated the probability of a tactical nuclear weapon being detonated by terrorists on U.S. soil in the next ten years as being 50 percent. The former chair of the 9/11 commission, Thomas Kean, cited these odds within a six-year time frame. These reports, in our view, are terrifying.

ACKNOWLEDGMENTS

We would like to thank many people for the contributions they made to this book. Foremost among them are the children and adults in Sri Lanka, who generously and patiently answered our questions, our colleagues, friends, and hosts who made the trip possible, and our able and generous translators, who served as guides to the culture and the island. All of you have shown the utmost kindness, even under difficult circumstances. Neither this book nor our understanding of the conditions that make youth believe that joining a terrorist group might be a good idea would be possible without your generosity. We hope we have done justice to your stories.

In addition to our friends in Sri Lanka, we want to acknowledge all those who work toward mutual understanding and acceptance in small everyday matters and in matters of great global importance, in the service of averting or ending war. And to those who work tirelessly to end the conditions that foster terrorism. These include aid workers, peacekeepers, diplomats, scientists, officials, and all those dedicated citizens who set about to make the world a better fairer place.

We thank our colleagues in the Society for Terrorism Research for inspiring our continued research efforts; at Endicott College, for encouraging continuing engagement with the concerns and people of Sri Lanka; at Massachusetts General Hospital, for challenging us to think beyond convention and understand these issues from a complex perspective; at the Center for Multicultural Training in Psychology, for constantly encouraging us to dare to see multiple points of view; and at Suffolk University, for ideas, support, and encouragement of our many projects. Most of all, of course, we thank our families, for their patience and support through long hours, and their understanding at moments when the topic we

were studying made us sad or temporarily discouraged. We know there were times when they would have rather had our attention, but instead they encouraged our research efforts.

We thank Debbie Carvalko, at Praeger, who had faith in us from start to finish, and who was always available to answer any questions, whether or not we knew the correct terminology to ask them! She consistently showed the most amazing mix of personal encouragement and professional competence.

Suffolk University, in Boston, Massachusetts, provided partial support for the development of this manuscript through a small faculty development grant to Alice LoCicero and conference travel stipends for both Alice LoCicero and Samuel Justin Sinclair.

GROWING UP IN WAR ZONES: CHILDREN AND THE COMMUNITIES THAT LOVE THEM

Endangered Children

The principal was dressed in a perfectly pressed light European-style suit. His face was clean and amazingly dry, as he was everyday, even when, as today, it was 105 degrees, sunny, and very, very humid, and even though air conditioning, in a school, was out of the question. He had perfect posture and could have been mistaken for a time-traveling twin of one of the models photographed for any of the decades-old textbooks on the shelves of this Sri Lankan school. He was not even paying attention to the heat, or the fan, as he paced in and out of its range, repeatedly phoning the young man, and getting no response. The effect was puzzling, as if the dignified principal had suddenly decided to be a different person—expressive, upset, rather than the calm and inscrutable self he had seemed to have spent most of his nearly sixty years cultivating. He phoned over and over again. Although it was broad daylight, and the young man was a steady, law-abiding citizen, very bright, and had never been in trouble, the principal explained, he was still at risk, simply because he was young, male, and of Tamil ethnicity. The principal was sure that if the young man did not return soon, he was gone for good, and it would be impossible to find out what happened to him; he would never be seen or heard from again.

The challenge the principal faced daily, he said, and had often said, is balancing between providing the young men opportunities to navigate and succeed in their world, on the one hand, and keeping them safe, on the other. "Like every parent," I thought, "except the stakes, and the odds, are different." Leaning toward showing trust that day, he had sent him on this very limited errand. Now, he could not hide behind the grooming, the posture, or the dignity. He was distraught, and it showed—consumed with the possibility that he had made the wrong decision.

After a few tortuous minutes of trying to continue our discussion about the challenges of educating children after a tsunami, and during a war, there were sounds outside, and the principal walked briskly to the window. Soon a healthy, handsome, alert young man—one who reminded me of many of my children's American friends when they were the same age—with his black hair and brown skin damp from sweat, holding a small sack, calmly walked in the door of the office, apologizing. The principal welcomed him back, his eyes a little wet and a little red. Regaining his composure only partially, his voice cracking a little, he told the young man that he had tried to call. The errand had taken a little longer than expected, the young man explained, and the cell phone had not been functioning. Later the principal told me what he, and others, believe: Sometimes "they" cut off the cell phone signal as another way of harassing "us." It took a moment to imagine how anyone with enough power to cut off the phone signal would want to hassle this principal. I wondered, for a moment, what entity he was referring to as "they."

This was one day when nothing devastating happened at *this* school. Every such day was viewed as lucky, a temporary tip of the balance toward survival. Some days tipped the other way, for no discernible reason. Even on good days, though, there was always the sobering thought that quite possibly, in some other nearby school, in some nearby village, on that day, a young boy did not come back. Some other boys, in the past, had not returned to this very school and the principal had no idea where they were. It is very likely that they were taken by the government of Sri Lanka, although they may have been taken by the LTTE, the Liberation Tigers of Tamil Eelam, also called the Tamil Tigers. The LTTE is believed to engage in conscription by kidnapping; the government is believed to imprison and kill young men when there is even the remotest possibility they might be supporting—or even considering joining—the LTTE, and possibly for other unknown reasons. It is believed the government does so with impunity. Most of the global community condemns the LTTE, and simultaneously believes the government's human rights record is seriously problematic (Human Rights Watch 2008, 79).[1] Recently the U.S. government cut military aid to Sri Lanka and will only restore it when the government demonstrates progress in the area of human rights. There are also factions that may or may not be part of the LTTE or the government. The situation is so devastating and so complex that it makes most ordinary citizens of the Western world throw up their hands and decide to think about something else.

Life in War-Affected Areas

But this was the very thing we had committed to thinking about: Life in a war-affected area, where some of the attacks include the planned death of the attacker, and where the victims are civilians. Indeed, we had agreed that thinking was not enough, and that one of us traveling to such an area was necessary if we

were to provide accurate and credible answers to the questions we had been working on for several years, including why a young person would sign up to be a terrorist who dies in an attack. We chose Sri Lanka because there is a long history of children fighting in a civil war that has lasted over twenty-five years. Sri Lanka is sometimes credited with (or condemned for) the first modern "suicide" or "martyr" attack. The children in Sri Lanka have never known peace, although they have known a brief cease-fire in 2002 and a brief period of cooperation and lack of fighting following the 2004 tsunami. We worked out our research questions, received approval from our university research review board, and set out to contribute to efforts of social scientists around the world to answer these essential questions. Once we had our answers, we collaborated with others, sharing our findings and what we made of them with the findings of other social scientists at international conferences, including the conference described in chapter 2.

I decided to go because my children are young adults and self-sufficient, and no one depended on me in the immediate sense of needing my day-to-day care, and because after speaking to many aid workers, journalists, and others who had recently visited the northeastern region of the island, I judged the risk to be acceptable in relation to the potential that some benefit to science would come of the trip.

Although it will be hard for many people to understand, and it took us a very long time to understand, this very way of thinking was parallel to some of the decisions made by voluntary child soldiers. My belief in the importance of knowledge led me to be willing to take some risks. I allowed myself to see my life in a balance, with risks to survival weighed out against a potential good for a community. As I learned over the next year, some of the young soldiers and terrorists we have wondered about make the same sorts of comparisons: they weigh their lives against what, in their thinking, misguided as it may be, may bring good to their communities.

I spent three weeks in Sri Lanka beginning May 24, 2007. A month or so before my departure, the LTTE was reported to have bombed a government air base outside Colombo. The main passenger airport schedule was, as a result, limited, causing rescheduling of some of my flights. I did not know of all the flight changes, and I arrived about five hours later than I had expected. My kind and patient hosts—people I had never met, but who were friends of friends—had simply waited. This was my first introduction to the kindness, generosity, and patience of most of the Sri Lankan people I met.

During the three weeks that I was in Sri Lanka, two International Committee of the Red Cross workers were kidnapped from a public train station and killed, a Mercy Corps worker was shot, and hundreds of ethnic Tamils were summarily rounded up in Colombo, put on buses, and brought to the northeastern part of the country, causing international protest. They were later returned to Colombo.

Also during that time period, there was a rail track explosion that wounded a few people. This was not an unusual amount of turmoil affecting civilians in Sri Lanka, an island about the size of West Virginia, with a population of about twenty million.

On the Ground

The trip from the airport to northeastern Sri Lanka was exciting and a bit hair-raising. Drivers go fast, the roads are not well-paved, and horns are used a great deal more than brakes. I learned later that there is some sort of courtesy code for one-lane roads, so drivers decide in advance who will go first, but before I knew that, it looked like whoever had the steeliest nerves boldly went ahead. In the middle of the night, we went through many villages where there was a great deal of activity. Children, adults, chickens, dogs, and cows were up and about. I later learned that this was due in part to the slight relief during the night from the extreme heat of each day.

There were numerous checkpoints between the airport and the northeastern part of the island. We went through most of them with no hassle. At one point, however, there was a long delay while the soldiers or police asked the males to leave the vehicle and spent quite a long time talking with them and examining their papers. It occurred to me that it would be quite a problem for me to figure out what to do if they were to be taken away. Eventually, we made it to our destination, and, I went to sleep under mosquito net, but only after double checking to be sure that what I was not hallucinating and that what I saw hopping out of the toilet tank was, indeed, a tiny frog.

Past Checkpoints, in Town

My luggage arrived a few days after I did, and in the interim, I needed a couple of articles of clothing. When I tagged along with someone going into town so that I could get these essentials, I brought a camera. But I did not take a single photograph—I was afraid to show a camera in front of the soldiers, a fear that the people who lived there thought was justified. It seemed there were soldiers everywhere, some looking quite nervous. So I never did take a photo in the town, although I took some in areas attractive to tourists. Unfortunately, there are virtually no tourists because of the war. During my trip, these areas were pathetically empty, despite their appeal.

If I had taken photos in the town, the photos would have looked like this: Old men with white hair and brown skin wearing white shirts and dhotis—cloth wrapped around their waists and legs—riding bicycles with one gear along the partially paved roads, balancing huge boxes full of bread they were delivering, as they navigated barriers and obstacles and checkpoints. Cows wandering along

on the streets, oblivious to their interference with three-wheelers carrying women in shimmering saris. The three-wheelers—open carriages balanced on motorcycle-engine-powered chassis—usually functioned as taxis and were driven exclusively by men, weaving seemingly perilously among much larger buses, vans, and trucks, so close that for the first few days I spent too much time gasping, waiting for the crash I was sure was imminent. (I never saw any crash or even scrape.) Motorcycles carried all sorts of people, sometimes one carried three or four people, sometimes a family with children. There were pedestrians dressed in bright colors, many carrying umbrellas against the glaring sun. Dogs were resting. An occasional beggar was sitting alone. Young women in tunics and pants, and older women in dresses, many carrying umbrellas to protect themselves from the sun, walked slowly. Children ran and laughed, and played. Many people of all sizes stood waiting as all the passengers of a bus on which they had been riding had their IDs checked by soldiers at one or another checkpoint. Sagging buildings, some that had been rendered totally useless by the tsunami, and others, appearing barely more functional, advertising food, pharmaceuticals, and computer training. Sturdier buildings with discreet signs designating them as government agencies or banks. Ditches were full of trash and rain water. Stores had wide open fronts, and, at small stands along the road here and there, vendors sold newspapers, coconuts, yogurt, fruit, rice, scarves, and toys. And everywhere, people were making do, one way or another. It looked like many other villages, in many other parts of the world, except for the rifle-carrying soldiers everywhere you turned. Some were in makeshift bunkers, consisting of bags of sand stacked up. Some soldiers, partially hidden behind bushes, above the road, held the rifle sights up to their eyes, ready to shoot. One pretended to be Rambo when he did not think anyone was watching. They were ubiquitous, but they were, collectively, just one reminder of the ever-present, tiring, enervating, reality of war.

There were seemingly endless beautiful beaches with transparent aqua water, all starkly empty. A very few hotels here and there were currently at about 5 percent occupancy, most of the occupants being tired, sunburned European aid workers. Occasionally, you could see a modern SUV with lettering indicating it carried UN employees. They drove quietly, and with their windows closed, because they, unlike everyone else, had air conditioning. Then again they, unlike anyone else, spent most of their hot sunny days dismantling and removing land mines. Workers from the United Nations and such organizations were not stopped at checkpoints, but every other vehicle or pedestrian might be stopped and searched by any of the soldiers. Sometimes the stops were cursory, but other times, they were lengthy, and the soldiers opened bags and asked many questions. Many times the soldiers appeared relaxed, but occasionally, probably when they had some reason to believe there was danger, they appeared anxious and on high alert. For most of my trip, I experienced little fear. The soldiers were courteous to me, and, I was told, were more courteous to the Tamils with whom I traveled because

of my presence. It was explained to me that most of the people of European descent were there to provide aid, and that I was presumed to be an aid worker, and therefore treated with courtesy. It seemed to me also possible that the soldiers and police at checkpoints were not in the habit of mistreating foreigners because the government did not want word of mistreatment getting into the international press. If that was their intent, they underestimated human rights groups, who were already well aware of the mistreatment of local Sri Lankan ethnic Tamils.

The people who lived there did not think the soldiers expected to find a terrorist. They thought the government wanted the soldiers to hassle the innocent ethnic Tamil citizens enough that they would be so fed up with war they would turn against the LTTE. That seemed to me to be unlikely, since they had not turned against the LTTE for the previous twenty-five years.

Across the Globe

When my three weeks were over, I was very glad to come home to the United States. And while America had not changed much, my view of it had changed a great deal. We will try to explain in this book how the lives of Americans are, even though we did not know it before, inextricably connected, in this twenty-first-century world, with the lives of Sri Lankans, and with the lives of people everywhere, including people we never even heard of, people whose lives may seem unimportant, and who seem to have no power to influence world events.

Americans are busy. What luxuries we have are often felt to be hard-won. There are daily challenges, what with every adult working—typically more than forty hours each week—and most raising children, and with trying to have a few minutes for oneself once in a while, and a few minutes of fun with your loved ones. We do not want to spend much time thinking about places like Sri Lanka. But when Americans and Europeans choose to ignore places like this, when it all seems too complex and depressing, and we decide to think about something else, we do so at our peril.

Sri Lanka, like many other parts of the world in the twenty-first century, is, for complex reasons, including the disappearances of young men and women, the poverty, the fear, and the enormous government-sanctioned discrepancies between the chances for a good future if you are Sinhalese as compared with the chances for a good future—or any future—if you are Tamil, an incubator for terrorism. When we choose not to consider, or care about, the amazingly beautiful, intelligent, well-mannered, endangered boys and girls of Sri Lanka and other such incubators, we are engaging in a dangerous game of pretend—pretending that the United States is invincible and the first world is separated from the third world by an impenetrable barrier. Further, we pretend that all we have to do is choose the right leader, and the leader will take care of all the worrying about what happens thousands of miles offshore.

In fact, the globe is small, we are all "on the ground," and leaders have not had much success in ending the conditions that foster terrorism, even when they have been able to block it for a while, or more dramatically and hopefully, resolve differences in a few specific places, such as Northern Ireland. It would be good if we, as global citizens, would awaken from complacency, allow ourselves to care, and decide to do something. It would be especially good if this happens before another attack forces us to do so. We who have some means and power, even if it is not much, must gather our means and power, and begin to understand and then find ways to intervene in the circumstances that create terrorism, if only for the survival of our own children and grandchildren, who, after all, will have to share this very small planet with those who have been privileged, and those who have not been privileged, with freedom, opportunity, education, and power.

Knowledge, Power, Action

Our goal, in this book, is to bring knowledge about terrorism to readers who have unanswered questions, and for whom the knowledge they desire to gain has not been readily available. We have done our own research to gain some knowledge, but we have also worked with other researchers around the world, in order to include knowledge that has been gained by those researchers, about the families and communities who raise children who become terrorists—choosing to be martyrs in their own eyes and the eyes of those who approve, or suicide attackers in the eyes of disapproving others. The work we are reporting here is the work of basic science, both theory and research. We have participated in efforts to facilitate the exchange of knowledge by creating an organization of researchers concerned with terrorism, and by co-sponsoring an international conference, which we report on in the next chapter.

This work is no more, or less, important than basic science involving proteins, genes, computer modeling, and nuclear fusion. With this knowledge, realistic and science-based decisions can be made, decisions that have some hope of success. The knowledge base of social science in this area is substantial, even though it is still evolving. Indeed, in the twenty-first century, attention to social science is critical if we—all seven billion of us humans—are to live together while avoiding having ethnic conflict turn into chaotic international violence, and without man-made disasters continuing their path of destruction until they consume our small planet.

Social Science of Youth and Terrorism

In this book, we describe our theory and research on youth who become terrorists, with an emphasis on the conditions of their families and communities that raise them. We build on fundamental developmental and ecological theories

of Jean Piaget, Lawrence Kohlberg, Michael Lamport Commons, Robert L. Selman, and Urie Bronfenbrenner, as well as contemporary research on adolescent cognitive development. We also rely on models of positive development, based on the work of Martin E. Seligman, and those referred to as "Youth Development" models. Successive chapters focus on the status of research on terrorism, and then on applications of psychological knowledge to terrorism. We include knowledge we have about the cognitive and social development of children, the environments provided by families, educational systems, belief systems, communities, nations, and international conditions.

We find ourselves venturing into territory seldom approached by social scientists, such as considering negative motivations of greed and hunger for power, alongside more positive motivations such as care, compassion, and altruism. We combine our knowledge and theory with the knowledge and theory being developed by other social scientists in other parts of the world, and we report, in chapter 2, on questions that are the focus of intensive, ongoing research, as well as questions about which there is already some agreement. At the end of the book, we make multiple suggestions about how ordinary Americans, as well as officials and professionals, can work to create and maintain communities that emphasize prevention, deterrence, and a potential for intervention, if needed, in our own communities, and in the global community.

THE SOCIAL SCIENCE OF TERRORISM

September 2007, Madrid: "I Declare This Conference Open"

The short drive along *Carretera de Rascafría* is likely to be punctuated by gazes and gasps—reactions to the extraordinary beauty of the hills and the almost dizzying excitement of the road's curves. Gaze up at the wrong moment—about one and a half kilometers out of town—and you are apt to miss the modest sign on a nearly hidden driveway. The sign announces *Residencia La Cristalera.* Inside, the staff—like docents—prepare to point you to its illustrious history—history you will momentarily be part of. From the trees nearby, the azure-winged magpies call out the joy of harvest in the *Sierra de la Nevadas,* their call a playful contrast with the quiet of the sleepy camouflage-toned inn. Especially in the early fall, the building, with the exception of the glass-walled dining wing from which it likely gets its name, nearly succeeds at blending into the hillside.

Residencia La Cristalera does not reach out and welcome you. Rather it stands self-contained and patient, if not indifferent, as you find your way to its hidden and unmarked entryway. The suites' and conference meeting halls' décor and design are subtle. Like the outside, and like the serious scholars it hosts, *La Cristalera* is modest. While inviting attention to the scholarship that takes place within its windowed walls, it eschews attention to itself. If you are expected here, you are warmly welcomed on entry by staff and hosts who seem to appear from nowhere and whose friendliness sharply contrasts with the reserved dignity of the center itself. Most international conferences have English as their official language, and some staff members are more fluent in English than others. Perhaps you find some other common language that works for you, but even if English is the only language in which you are fluent, they can meet your needs. Arrive just on time, and the center is apt to be resuming activity after a brief

dormant state. It is as if you have arrived at a museum on a quiet day at opening time. You easily forgive its somewhat worn appearance; in fact you may even welcome it, since it is fitting that nothing should have changed. For decades, scholars have met here to collaborate, share their new knowledge, and find ways to make the world better. Reminders of this history hang on the walls—photos showing groups of scientists, physicians, and scholars taking a moment from their work to pose in the rose garden in sunlight or darkness. There are signs that those scientists know how to play hard and let off steam—the unheated swimming pool, the ping-pong table, the casually maintained tennis and handball courts.

In late September, the midday brings a welcome warmth and you can take the short walk on the road into the town called *Miraflores,* the midday sun reminding you that a short time ago, the days were longer and saturated with warm sun and the gardens in full colorful bloom. But you must be agile, brave, or foolhardy to take that walk, since there are no sidewalks along the narrow winding road. At midday, you easily remember that only a few months from now the roses will be in bloom again. But then evening comes early, and with the darkness a chilly reminder that the branches with roses past their prime will be barren and then snow-covered before the promise of next year's young buds appears.

Interdisciplinary Analyses of Aggression and Terrorism

In September 2007, *La Cristalera* hosted sixty-five or so of the world's researchers on the social science of aggression and terrorism. The conference was open to any registrant, and invitations were extended to those scholars who were already contributing to the analysis of this vexing problem.[1] The researchers spent three days together, reading papers, discussing findings, agreeing, disagreeing, creating and strengthening collaborations while eating meals and drinking tea, coffee, and spirits, joking, and playing games together. Conference organizers and conferees agreed that questions and issues relevant to terrorism are not solvable by those in one discipline alone, but are so complex as to require teams and collaborators to analyze the conditions and persons involved from many perspectives. Disciplines represented included physics, law, medicine, psychology, political science, biology, military science, and journalism. Outside conference time, some attendees stayed up late for discussions. Some spent lunch hours hiking into the wooded mountain parks. Some played basketball or tennis—lawn or table. Security for the conference was high, and—as it should be—nearly invisible.

Like most professional conferences in the United States, this one had dinner and a keynote address at its opening, and it also included a more formal, traditional, weighty reminder that there was serious work to be done: In a ritual linking those studying aggression and terrorism to all the scholars who had met here in the past—those who studied medicine, geology, nuclear weapons, and many other things—the conferees were welcomed by their own vibrant and friendly

conference chairs, followed by a sincere and formal city official, and some serious and dutiful representatives of the *Universidad Autónoma de Madrid* (Autonomous University of Madrid), one of whom formally declared the conference "open."

Update on the Social Science of Aggression and Terrorism

During the next three days, conferees—old, young, male, female, representing several kinds of cultures and religions, and from several continents—shared their hard-earned understandings and knowledge about various aspects of aggression and terrorism in the context of contemporary world conditions and conflicts. Many had been studying these issues long before the terrorist attacks in the United States on September 11, 2001. Some lived in, and others had traveled to, places of unrest, and had researched the circumstances firsthand. Many were concerned about nuclear weapons, and some had been so concerned for decades. Like all researchers and journalists, the scholars addressed questions of what, when, where, how, who, and why. The geography of terrorism and concerns about it in the twenty-first century is broad and complex, involving multiple locations and including every continent. Scholars are variously concerned about understanding its victims and its perpetrators, about stopping or reducing it, and about reducing its impact on affected communities. Some researchers in attendance simply wanted to make an intellectual and scientific contribution to this vexing world problem, while others felt a deep personal sense of urgency, believing their loved ones, and human civilization as we know it, to be at imminent risk. There were scholars who studied individuals, groups, communities, cultures, countries, and relationships between countries or between a country and a nongovernment group. Some studied only children engaged in terrorism; others adults; others only women. Some studied cyber-terrorism. Some were particularly interested in understanding those who deliberately and planfully die in a terrorist action.

The Questions

Basic science can rarely be hurried. Still, at the end of three days, when, in another formal ceremony, the conference was declared closed, conferees were able to define several fundamental questions in need of answers that will help policymakers and citizens know what to do about terrorism. The answers, they agreed, are not in. Although some of the conferees are hard at work on them, and some researchers are likely to dispute the unresolved status of these key questions, the sense of participants at this meeting was that research has simply not gotten far enough to rule out all but one of the multiple possible answers to any of these questions.

Agreeing on the critical questions, however, and defining the issues that make them hard to answer, is a huge first step. After listing the questions here, we will

discuss the issues and perspectives involved in attempts to answer the questions from our own perspective. We will refer to discussions at the conference, all the time realizing that we are reporting only from our own point of view, not that of others. The first and most fundamental question possible begins the list: What is terrorism? Then there is a related question, also quite basic: Why do people engage in terrorist actions? A corollary to that question is whether those who engage in terrorist actions are mentally fit. Emerging from those fundamental questions is the important consideration as to whether grievances—some of them legitimate—are a real and serious contributing cause of terrorism, and whether addressing legitimate grievances that exist and that, in some instances at least, appear to fuel terrorism would prevent or reduce terrorist actions. A corollary question to that is whether, once a terrorist act has taken place, the group responsible should have their grievances addressed. This question becomes important when considering another question: Once terrorist actions or general violence have taken place, what are the steps and obstacles to steps that must be taken to resolve conflicts and bring communities to a more peaceful state.

Quite a different set of questions emerges with regard to the impact of terrorist actions on a community. Most conferees were in agreement that some attention must be made to the issue of mitigating the psychological impact of terrorism so that a terrorist action does not upset or even destabilize an entire community. But how do you measure the impact? Are current measures, that mostly focus on trauma, sufficient? Are some communities more resilient than others? If so, why? And how, once you have measured the psychological impact of a terrorist event, can you assist the surviving victims toward a speedy recovery, or at least a speedy return to their former status as contributing members of the community?

What Is Terrorism?

Amazing as it may seem, there is, as yet, no generally accepted definition of terrorism. Even the United Nations has not defined it. Some people think they know it when they see it, but there have recently been events variously claimed by some experts to be, and by other experts not to be, terrorism. Conferees noted that there were scores of definitions available, and called for general agreement on a working definition. The word "terrorism" itself is considered likely to be a key to choosing a definition: Terrorists want to cause serious widespread fear (terror)—even more than they want to cause widespread destruction. Researchers, including some at the conference, refer to a statement made by Brian Jenkins, who put it succinctly: "Terrorists want a lot of people watching, not a lot of people dead."[2] Beyond that, most, but not all, researchers seem to agree that for an attack to be rightfully called "terrorism" it must target civilians. Yet there are exceptions—groups most governments would agree are terrorists sometimes only target military or government officials—or at least claim to. In colloquial usage,

terrorism is usually limited to nongovernment entities. Yet governments not infrequently engage in activities that qualify as terrorism on many criteria.

As I wrote this chapter, another incident illustrating the difficulty of defining terrorism occurred. I learned that former Prime Minister Benazir Bhutto has been assassinated in Pakistan. It appears from initial reports that the assassin shot her, then detonated a bomb that killed both the assassin and many others. Was her assassination an instance of terrorism? (Suicide terrorism?) Some might argue not, since its apparent target was Bhutto, a political figure participating in a protest rally. Bystanders who also died might be considered by some to be in the category of "collateral damage." This is in contrast to attacks targeting people shopping at a mall, dining in a café, or arriving at work. Yet a few days later, the attack was blamed on al Qaeda affiliates. Does such an affiliation make it more likely that the attack will be seen as terrorism?

Many conferees thought that an agreed-upon definition of terrorism would be useful, even if it were imperfect, and even if it were later revised. An agreed-upon definition would have the advantage that all other social science researchers would know what was—and was not—being talked about when the word terrorism was used. The scientists had heard—too often it seemed—the sentence that often derails attempts to define terrorism: "One man's terrorist is another man's freedom fighter." To some, the assassin who killed Bhutto may be a "freedom fighter." Such differing perspectives are illustrated even in fictional terrorism. For example, when Carmen, a seventeen-year-old member of the terrorist group that holds hostages in the novel, *Bel Canto,* says of her mission, "I work to free the people." The Red Cross intermediary in the novel is weary of such common and, he feels, vague statements.

Conferees clearly believed that even if it is true that one man's terrorist is another man's freedom fighter, this should not stand in the way of getting a consensus or at least a majority opinion among researchers on what constitutes terrorism. We believe that part of the problem of defining terrorism is that, apart from incidents described as terrorism, it does not have an ongoing concrete reality. That is, it does not exist separate from events, other than in thought—or dread. There are terrorist actions, or actions that may be referred to as terrorism, but there is no terrorism apart from actions or events. And the events referred to as terrorism are highly disparate. When the authorities say they are protecting people against terrorism, it is against the imagined terrorism that might happen. This is unlike, say, protecting people against anthrax or the AIDS virus, both of which are definable and exist, in a somewhat tangible (if unstable) form. Moghaddam Assaf, discussing the difficulties in defining suicide terrorism, suggests using terms like "mission" or "attack" rather than terrorism. Perhaps such usage would be helpful in the short run, but the term terrorism is probably here to stay for a while, so having a clear sense of what researchers, at least, mean when they use the term may be helpful.

Defining Terrorism

We insert here a brief overview of discussions of terrorism, including its history, as it is typically understood by social scientists. This overview addresses the lack of consensus as to what it means or from where it comes.

The term *terrorism* has been around for some time, with some experts dating its origin back to the 1790s during the French Revolution and the "Reign of Terror" carried out by Maximilien Robespierre. Others date this phenomenon back even further to AD 48, when a Jewish faction, the Zealots, employed a terrorist campaign against the Romans. Given the complexity involved in defining terrorism, and the heterogeneity in terms of the tactics employed, underlying rationale for using terrorism as a strategy, and the groups who have engaged these methods, it is understandable that there has not, as of yet, been a consensus as to its meaning.

Another complicating factor related to the difficulties in defining this term has been the issue of whether there is a state sponsor backing the "terrorism" campaign, or whether these groups are operating without a government's backing. In those instances where there is a state sponsor, do these tactics qualify as terrorism or as an act of war perpetrated by a standing government? Most people who use this term today refer to the latter group. However, as some have pointed out, state-sponsored terrorism has been responsible for the vast majority of deaths when compared to nonstate groups. Clark McCauley has estimated the ratio to be about 260 to 1, or roughly 170 million people killed by state-sponsored groups (e.g., Stalin, Hitler, and Mao) and roughly 500,000 killed by nonstate groups.

More recently, nonstate terrorist groups like al Qaeda have risen to prominence with the attacks of September 11, 2001, and have given the term new meaning for those living within the United States. Prior to 9/11, it could be safely argued that it was *not* a national priority. Interestingly, although the term "terrorism" is commonly used in today's nomenclature, there has been considerable debate as to its meaning. Recently, the former Secretary General of the United Nations, Kofi Annan, called for a universal definition of terrorism for purposes of structuring an international response. According to the BBC News Agency, the new UN proposal "calls terrorism any act intended to intimidate a population or to compel a government or an international body to act." The recent debate over the use of this term has centered on the Palestinian–Israeli conflict, creating a stalemate within the United Nations since 1996 in formally defining terrorism. Whereas many have viewed the Palestinian struggle as an organized resistance to occupation, many others have viewed their tactics as being "terrorist" in nature, where noncombatants are targeted for purposes of affecting some change in governmental policy.

The ensuing debate has thus centered around the "one person's terrorist is another person's freedom fighter" line of argument, making such terms relative in nature. Using terms such as "terrorism," then, has become a double-edged

sword. However, given that many in Western society and especially in those places that have been attacked (e.g., Madrid, Bali, London, Indonesia, and the United States) ascribe a particular meaning to it, we believe the term can and should be used in academic and scientific inquiry. Just because there are groups of people who do not see these as acts of "terrorism" does not mean that there are not many others out there who have experienced it as terrorism.

One of the primary factors fueling this debate has been the evolution of terrorism over time. In his discussion of the psychology of terrorism, Jerrold Post differentiated between two different forms of "modern terrorism," which have dominated since the early 1970s. He argued that the catalyst for modern terrorism was when the Israeli Olympic Village was seized by the Black September Terrorists in 1972 in Munich, Germany. As a consequence, there was an incredible international television audience that watched the events unfold, elucidating for different groups the power that such acts had on garnering attention for one's political cause. According to him, the two types of terrorist movements that were most prominent in the early 1970s were the *social revolutionary* and the *nationalist-separatist* terrorists. The former was engaged in resisting and overthrowing the regimes of their parents' generation, and used terrorism to enact revenge for the perceived failures for which these regimes were held responsible. The latter was carrying on the mission of their parents' generation, which was focused on separating themselves from those regimes in place and forming new states based on these minority identities (e.g., the Irish Republican Army). Both groups were politically motivated and were intent on gaining attention from the West to further their cause.

Then in the 1980s and 1990s, the second type of modern terrorist movement began to emerge, driven by extremist interpretations of Islam. According to Post, these groups were not motivated for political reasons, nor did they seek recognition from Western society. Rather, their goals were to eliminate Western secular influence from their lands. The only recognition they cared about was that from their God. Post argues that currently these groups, including al Qaeda and its many splinter organizations, pose a severe danger to contemporary society, because of the lengths to which they were willing to go in achieving their goals.

For the purpose of discussion, Jessica Stern's (2003, p. 1) definition of terrorism is used. We want to be clear here that terrorism does not actually exist apart from terrorist actions. Although we follow Stern's definition, we believe we are defining acts, rather than a movement or other reality definable on its own, apart from incidents or actions. "First, terrorism is aimed at non-combatants.... Second, terrorists use violence for dramatic purposes: instilling fear in the target audience is often more important than the physical result. This deliberate creation of dread is what distinguishes terrorism from simple murder or assault..." (p. 1). So, for example, some have labeled the 1984 attacks on the U.S. Marine Corps barracks in Beirut a "terrorist" attack. Based on the operational definition we are using, we would not because noncombatants were not targeted.

Finding a Prototypical Terrorist

If terrorism is defined as an act of violence whose goal is "drama" and "dread" and whose victims are noncombatants, does that help us to know what a terrorist is?

Like terrorism, terrorists are defined by an action or sequence of events. No one is a terrorist until he or she has done a terrorist action. Unlike terrorism, though, someone who has performed a terrorist action can be pointed to and has an existence after the action. (Even if it is a successful suicide/martyr terrorist action, there is an existence in memory. To some it is the memory of a martyr; to others, a killer.) For those who do not die in an attack, life after terrorism, for youthful terrorists, at least, need not be solely determined by their history of having participated in terrorist actions. Many are capable of full reintegration into communities, and capable of leading productive, nonviolent adult lives, although some lead lives of continued violence. This makes the term "terrorist" a potentially transient role, like "soldier" or "student."

Psychologists have shown that many concepts are best defined—or at least first defined—by comparison with a prototype. When you see a puppy, even if it is a breed of puppy you have never seen before, you do not need to count paws, check for a wet nose, or wait to hear it bark. You "know" it is a young dog because you can compare it to other puppies you have seen, and that type of comparison happens so fast you do not even know it is happening. It is quite amazing to realize that we also rapidly compare it to other nonpuppies (e.g., cats, mice, or toasters) we have seen, and rule categories out—in less than a heartbeat. At that point, a definition of a puppy would be something like "a puppy-like creature, reminiscent of other creatures called puppies." The same sort of thinking comes into play when we see a graduation, for example. With a few cues, we can easily distinguish a graduation from a musical, a wedding, and a political rally. We do not need to make a list of all the factors that make it a graduation, though our minds are rapidly processing those.

This automatic process does not, as yet, lead to a reliably shared image or idea for terrorism or terrorists. It seems to us that, in the United States, at least two events currently compete to become the most likely prototype for terrorism: The events of September 11, 2001 is one contender, and the other is the kind of event where a lone bomber destroys a civilian area in Israel—perhaps a bus, a mall, or a café—killing himself in the process. These two events are different enough, and the perpetrators are different enough, that attempts to formulate a shared American prototype from them have so far faltered. When we think of the possible prototypical events available to an international group of researchers, we include the Madrid train bombings or the London subway bombings, the many acts of violence toward civilians that have taken place in Iraq, the Oklahoma City bombing, and the various bombings of embassies in Africa, events in Bali, Colombia, Sri Lanka, and Saudi Arabia, and more—all called

terrorism, and it is not so surprising that no prototype has yet led to consensus on what terrorism is and is not, or what a terrorist is like. No wonder, then, that no definition has been agreed upon.

Prototypes of Terrorists

If no prototypical event as yet become a widely shared basis for a definition of terrorism, is it possible that a prototypical terrorist could emerge? Many have tried to describe, define, profile, or diagnose terrorists, but these attempts have led to some disputes, often with evidence of more terrorists who are exceptions to the profiles proposed than those who fit, thus failing to lead to an agreed-upon definition. In spite of multiple interviews, case studies, and applications of scientific and forensic knowledge, no prototypical terrorist is agreed upon. Perhaps this is due to extreme variations among terrorists. If the two contenders for prototypical terrorist event are the events of September 11 and a bombing of a café or mall in Israel, perhaps the two contenders for Americans' terrorist prototypes are Osama bin Laden—or perhaps Mohammed Atta—and a young, nameless, undistinguished devout fellow who has been recruited at his mosque in Palestine with the promise of special status, money for his family, and virgin wives and a special place in Paradise, as well as automatic entry into heaven for dozens of his family and friends upon their deaths. This young devout fellow, who has had some training and has been taught to believe in the lack of humanity of Israelis, and perhaps Americans, too, is not otherwise apt to be special. Indeed, those who stand out would be excluded. The contrast between a wealthy, competent, smart, radical Islamist middle-aged adult (bin Laden) who is married and has children, has been engaged in planning and executing large operations, both humanitarian and destructive, and who has overseen large-scale battlefronts where many of his soldiers have died, and a poor, devout undistinguished teenager from an undistinguished family who has been recruited to do nothing special other than blow himself up in the midst of others, does not easily lead to a single prototype. Add in multiple other terrorist images, such as Dhanu, the first LTTE female suicide bomber who killed Rajiv Gandhi in 1991, the Chechen terrorists, and the U.S. homegrown terrorists, Timothy McVeigh and Terry Nichols, and it is not so hard to see why a consensus definition of terrorist has not been possible among Americans.

Most important for our work, neither bin Laden, nor the youthful, devout, undistinguished youth who may be the typical candidate for a Palestinian, or even more broadly of Islamic youthful terrorists in various locations are much like the typical adult or child in most parts of the world who become members of a group generally recognized as "terrorists." Indeed, the typical child who is a member of a group that engages in terrorist actions, and who might engage in terrorist actions himself or herself, is more like a typical child soldier, even if

he or she at some point planfully dies in a terrorist action. Such children are often trained to be, and think of themselves as, members of militia, who may or may not be chosen for various special assignments, including those in which they will die. Some have joined voluntarily, out of belief in the cause, which is, often, freedom for their people. Others have been kidnapped or threatened with punishment or death of their families if they do not join.

Social Scientists Describing Child Terrorists

In the past, enthusiasm for the power of social science sometimes led to studies where the well-being of the people it studied was sacrificed for the purpose of acquiring knowledge. At present, social science researchers tend to be very cautious. As a result, the requirements of social science and common ethical practice limit the kinds of descriptions that social scientists can write about actual living child soldiers or those who have engaged in violent actions, even terrorism. While a combination of many such case studies might lead to a prototype, publication of detailed case studies could put the children at risk of punishment by adults who disapproved of their cooperation with researchers. Research review boards, designed to monitor research in the interests of those being studied, are likely to prevent the very kind of research that might help provide direct, scientific answers to questions about typical child terrorists, even if the children were willing to provide the data needed. Indeed, researchers are bound by such strict rules that few even try to arrange interviews of children who are terrorists or even members of militia. If they do, they will not be describing actual individuals in detail.

That is not to say there are no studies of children who engage in terrorist actions. Indeed, there are some exceptionally carefully done social science studies that include interview data from children who are members of militias considered to be terrorist organizations. (See Keairns 2003, for example.) These studies together with reports from nongovernmental humanitarian organizations indicate that children become members of militias for a variety of reasons, including commitment to the cause, searching for a community, escaping from difficult circumstances, and, in many cases, they join because of coercion or threat. There are also (nonsensational) journalistic descriptions of children who are or were terrorist organizations (Briggs 2005; Mitchell 2006). And there are video documentaries that feature former child soldiers who might have engaged in terrorism, as they reenter their communities (Ahadi and Stoltz 2005). Recently, a biography of a former child soldier, Ishmael Beah (2007), who fought in a civil war in Sierra Leone, has been very well received. We learn from all these sources that child soldiers are a diverse lot, with various motives, demographics, and life histories. No simple profile will do.

Psychologist and author Erik Erikson (1954, p. 51) used a fictional character, Dr. Isak Borg, to illustrate the psychological processes of old age. He justified

doing so by reference to the limitations placed on social scientists such that "the necessity to guard their subject's privacy, while attempting to prove as logical and trustworthy their method of selecting their 'data'. . .may well make, on occasion, for more distortion than clarification" (p. 240). Similar concerns lead us to refer to fictional child terrorists, along with scientific accounts. We describe three specific characters, then a group of characters portrayed in one screenplay. A widely known classical fictional terrorist is the character Chen in Malraux's (1934) novel, *Man's Fate*, which drew on a failed Communist revolution in Shanghai in 1927. Chen is a terrorist who is strongly affected by his role as assassin, and who himself dies in a failed attempted suicide mission. A twenty-first-century terrorist, Ahmad, was created by John Updike for his novel, *Terrorist*. Updike's story takes place in northern New Jersey (a city with the fictional name of New Prospect that is a lot like Paterson) and seventy years after Chen. It tells a story of an American adolescent of mixed heritage who identifies himself as Muslim, and devoutly takes the Koran at its literal word, being groomed and recruited by his Imam, who himself is a tool of Islamic jihadists, to perform an act of potentially enormous destruction—blowing up the Lincoln Tunnel. Ahmad is very much like one of the prototypes described earlier—the young, devout, undistinguished Palestinian. Updike reminds us that the key factors leading to such a child performing a terrorist act may be present in the United States.

Several prototypes of child terrorists are included in Ann Patchett's *Bel Canto*. The events in that book were inspired by a real life terrorist event that took place in Peru in 1996; that event, like the novel, centered on hostage-taking. The militia group's characters are credible. She portrays them as real adolescents with personal challenges. The character Carmen reflects the complexity of being a young girl engaged with a terrorist group: Such engagement offers excitement, opportunity, sometimes improved access to basic resources such as food and health care,[3] as well as very real (if, at times, ignored) danger.

Let us compare, for a moment, the characters Carmen, in *Bel Canto*, and Ahmad, in *Terrorist*. Ahmad is close to the American prototype of a youthful terrorist who planfully dies in a terrorist action, a "suicide bomber." Carmen might be the best-known fictional child character who becomes a member of a terrorist organization. She first appears disguised as a boy. She is beautiful, smart, spunky, poor, uneducated, and from a small village in a poor country where there is ongoing political strife. She is seventeen years old, a member of an indigenous group, and religious—or at least she prays. But her religion seems not to have motivated her in joining the militia. Being a soldier/terrorist has brought her an interesting, and very likely more exciting, life than she would otherwise have had, while it has taken her away from her family. There are gains for her, including greater knowledge of the world and an opportunity for lifestyle that is not conventional, especially for a girl. Whether she was kidnapped or volunteered may or may not be important—it is not clear to the reader. What is clear is that there has been a

trade-off. She now lives an exciting life, that life brings costs, risks, and benefits. One cost is that she has to obey her general, even if she is ordered to scare or hurt others. Although the novel portrays a rather low level of violence, a somewhat incompetent group of terrorists, and a seemingly inevitable building of alliances across groups, inside the vice-president's house where the guests have been taken hostage, there are moments when a militia general orders the children to interact with the hostages in a way that engenders fear. The reader, like the characters, stays inside the house or on the grounds, and is made to be only dimly aware of what is going on outside. Carmen likes it there, and is willing for everyone to stay. "Would it be so bad…??" she asks. In the end, the risks associated with being a child soldier/terrorist becomes clear. While some may take the ending as a lesson that Carmen made the wrong decision in joining a terrorist group, others might argue that it was worth taking some risks to escape other inevitable risks to her—like the risks and extreme costs to most children around the world who live in countries engaged in a civil war: loss of loved ones, poverty, illiteracy, displacement, and limited opportunity. This, of course, makes it sound as if the children make a calculated rational decision, weighing costs and benefits of joining or not joining, which is unlikely, especially given what is known about adolescent reasoning. (See the discussion of adolescent reasoning in chapter 3 of this book.)

Both Carmen and Ahmad must address, for themselves, issues of growing up, of sexuality and lust, and of the ethics of their unconventional choices. But neither Carmen nor Ahmad express any hesitation or unclarity about the rightness of their choices. Even when Carmen develops a secret relationship with Gen, the translator, and then secretly assists the hostages, she does not express any doubt about either her role in the militia or her role with the hostages. And even when Ahmad changes his mind and decides not to blow up the Lincoln Tunnel, he does not seem to entertain mixed feelings. Rather he sees his new decision as fulfilling the wishes of Allah, just as he had earlier seen blowing up the tunnel as doing so. This lack of interest, or perhaps ability, to simultaneously entertain two conflicting points of view, while choosing a course of action, we have argued in an article on terrorist leaders (LoCicero and Sinclair 2008), is a developmental limitation. The kind of thinking that leads to such certainty in the point of view and in the actions one takes is necessary (though not sufficient) for engagement in terrorist actions. Once someone can recognize that two points of view both have potential validity, it is a short step to understanding that his or her own and his or her enemy's viewpoints each have merit to the person holding them. With that recognition, a terrorist action becomes far less likely.

Ahmad, by contrast with Carmen, has access to an education. His mother is a professional woman, and Jack, his guidance counselor, urges him to attend college. He does not seem to give college any thought, however, as he has already agreed to accept a job arranged for him by the Imam. Ahmad is characterized as aloof from the students and teachers in his high school, believing them to be

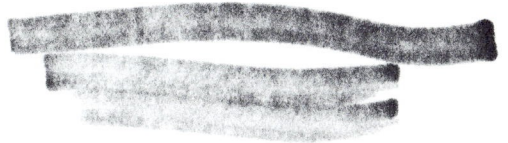

godless hypocrites, whose actions may be a threat to his own purity and an offense to Allah. He is thus a candidate to become a victim of older men who would take advantage of his youth, his devoutness, his competence, and his reliability. In this way, he is similar to one of the likely candidates for prototype child terrorist. He is not part of any militia, and not privy to any larger plan. He has only one mission, and his training for it has little to do with any conventional military or fitness training. Updike's contribution to the young Islamic terrorist prototype is giving readers access to Ahmad's innermost thoughts and emotions—making him understandable, and even a sympathetic character—and showing that he is a willing terrorist because he has been manipulated by adults. His actions can be understood in relation to his religious beliefs and to his adolescent thinking and emotions.

Although American media may be more likely to report on terrorists like Ahmad, reminiscent of Islamic anti-American, antisecularist, and anti-Israeli sentiments, social scientists who have studied terrorism around the world would be more likely to say that most of the children who carry out terrorist actions are far more like Carmen, who was recognized as having some strengths and talents, and who, due to the horrendous realities of ongoing war, somehow got recruited or coerced into a militia. Most youthful terrorists' understanding of their role is local, rather than global, and working to "free the people" is more likely the motivation than avenging global secularism or impurity in the Western world. Like Ahmad, Carmen has been manipulated, and like Ahmad she believes in and shows loyalty to those who have manipulated her.

Many Americans have become familiar with the ugliness of war involving children from the critically acclaimed film *Blood Diamond,* portraying war financed by diamond trade in Sierra Leone, a painful film to watch.

British playwright Robin Soans has created multiple, mostly nameless, mostly young, terrorists for the play *Talking to Terrorists* that opened in 2005. The director and cast of Soans's play had, indeed, talked with terrorists, in order to understand and better portray them. In the play, the children speak about atrocities committed and about how they were coerced to participate in terrorist activities. A character representing aid organization personnel tells of the overwhelming need and the limited resources to meet it.

Documentary filmmaker Beate Arnestad and producer Morton Daae have created the film *My Daughter, the Terrorist.* The filmmaker was allowed to film and interview two members of the LTTE elite Black Tigers, those groomed for missions in which they intentionally die. The young women she interviews are quite proud of their status. They describe learning to obey orders and also the power of a small number of Tigers to cause a considerable impact. The mother of one of the young women is also interviewed.

It seems to us that most Americans lack broad knowledge, and thus are apt to imagine that all child terrorists are like those who are recruited to die in order to

kill and scare Israelis and Americans. This is likely because the American commercial media—source of contemporary knowledge for most Americans—portray only children who become terrorists in the Middle East, rather than worldwide. (Quite possibly, this is because of a perception that there are more media consumers with interest in the Middle East than in other parts of the world.) In order to increase the range of images of child terrorists, one can go to the Internet to find information about child soldiers and child terrorists in parts of the world other than the Middle East. There Americans can find international media sources, including sources from the EU, Asia, and elsewhere, and in that way can learn about children engaged in ethnic violence in Sri Lanka, Africa, or Latin America. It is the complexity of including all child terrorists in one prototype that makes it hard to define children who are terrorists, just as it is the complexity of including all attacks considered by some to be terrorism in one prototype that makes it hard to define terrorism.

In the Meantime: Proposal for a Consensus Model

An analogous situation existed in psychiatry with respect to various loosely defined diagnostic categories until leaders in its field decided it would be better to have a set of shared diagnoses with criteria that they all could accept, even if they were not 100 percent in agreement and did not have 100 percent accurate clinical tests for these diagnoses. After all, they reasoned, if new knowledge is developed, the criteria could later be changed. This was working definition by consensus—still the basis of the series of Diagnostic and Statistical Manuals—now the DSM IV-TR is in use, soon to be replaced by the DSM-V. Each volume reflects changes and adjustments based on the latest research. Yet, at a given time, all psychiatrists, by common agreement, at least mean the same thing when they refer to someone who has a disorder such as schizophrenia. Terrorism needs such a working definition if we are to continue using the word.

What Causes Someone to Become a Terrorist?

This is one point on which there was a great deal of disagreement at the conference: The question of why one person engages in terrorist actions and another does not. Some attendees believed that only people who fit a category of disease or severe distress—having suffered severe abuse or neglect, or who are neurologically compromised, psychologically disturbed, or psychopathic—become terrorists. That is, they believe there is a fatal internal personal flaw of some kind that must be present for someone to kill innocent people. According to this theory, everyone who becomes a terrorist is, even before they act, in one category, and everyone who does not is in another category. Figure out how to make a good sort and you can stop terrorism by confining those with the flaw,

and perhaps engaging in advance intervention with those who are future terrorists. Such a theory is comforting, in part, because it suggests that no radical changes in the social order need be made. Rather, we need to do a better job at prediction and control, in the strict scientific sense. Predict who is going to become a terrorist and control their behavior so that they do not terrorize others.

At what seems to be the other end of the spectrum are those who say that terrorists are ordinary people whose bad fortune, lack of hope, lack of outlet for publicizing their point of view, and legitimate social grievances bring them to an act of violence out of desperation. That is, without a means to bring attention to a terrible plight and the plight of one's people, any of us, under the worst of circumstances, could become a terrorist. Any of us could do actions that we now see as too horrendous for words, if the right (or wrong) social and political conditions exist. This theory is less comforting. It suggests that some social changes are needed, and social changes are much harder to implement, and take longer to become effective.

Terrorism and Altruism

Actually, the idea that, legitimate or not, grievances of sufficient magnitude would lead anyone to engage in terrorism is not really at the other end of the spectrum from the idea that engaging in terrorist actions is a result of personal deficits. At the opposite end of that spectrum is the belief that those who become terrorists are not the sickest, nor the most vulnerable, but the most loving, compassionate, and altruistic, though misguided. According to this idea, terrorists risk, or even planfully end, their own lives, in order to do an action they believe will bring good to a larger social group. A girl soldier from Sri Lanka, describing her reasons for joining, quoted by Keairns, says,

> When I was about 12 years old I began to feel for all those people who were displaced and were coming from all over the areas. This and other incidents that people spoke about made me feel sad. Some schools were broken; we had no school and no freedom. I saw some people who were brought to the hospital; they were cut and maimed by the enemy/army. I knew some children who had lost both their parents and their life became so difficult overnight.

They will fight, and perhaps increase their chances of dying young so that others may have a chance for a better life. This idea, like the idea that every terrorist is disordered, has the advantage of suggesting that we might be able to predict and prevent terrorism by identifying those at risk of engaging in it. But it has the less comforting aspect that we cannot quite consign terrorism to the mentally ill or disordered. We must, instead, confront a somewhat amorphous question

about whether altruism and caring for others is a form of disturbance. And if not, we are left with acknowledging that at least those altruistic persons who choose martyrdom perceive a situation in which their loved ones are suffering and where desperate action is called for. This reason for engaging in terrorism is disturbing for another reason—one that most people will not want to discuss: If terrorists are altruistic and acting in a way that they believe will be good for their families, isn't the motivation of the terrorist awfully close to the motivation of those who join legitimated government military forces? They, too, care deeply for their group; they, too, want to make or keep their families safe. And they, too, cause damage to others, including sometimes civilians, when they think it is necessary for the ends their leaders have defined. Indeed, according to many social science experts on terrorism, the largest number of civilian deaths from terrorism in the twentieth century were the result of government-sponsored terrorism, carried out by official government forces, under the auspices of Hitler, Mao, and Stalin (McCauley 2004, p. 3).

Distinguishing Legitimate Militaries from Terrorist Groups

In some societies, then, the key difference often used to distinguish terrorism from legitimate military has been violated. That difference is that those forces we can call "terrorist" are likely to plot to kill civilians as a way of getting their ends met, while those who are legitimate military only kill civilians either by accident or as an unfortunate side effect of attempts to kill opposing combatants. History provides evidence of exceptions: Times when legitimated military forces have been ordered to kill civilians. In fuzzier situations, legitimate military may destroy a village or community where they believe there may be one or a few opposing combatants hiding; here the line between terrorists and legitimate military gets awfully close to blurring. Perhaps the looming blurry line is yet another reason that terrorism is so difficult to define.

What About Legitimate Grievances?

Another area where there was quite a bit of interest and discussion, and limited agreement, is this: What about the grievances that terrorist groups claim are the reason for their actions? How should the international community acknowledge that legitimate grievances exist? Should there be attempts to ameliorate all legitimate grievances? Who is to define what is a legitimate grievance? When a grievance is legitimate, but a heinous action has been committed, should the grievance still be addressed? These questions can cause divisions reflecting ethical concerns. The scientific question here is clear: Could early discussion and amelioration of grievances prevent terrorist actions? Here again, a larger question was looming, but it has barely been approached: Given that the world's wealth is so unevenly divided,

and the world's power is so unevenly divided, and given that such uneven division is often among the grievances causing terrorist actions, is redistribution of wealth necessary for prevention of terrorism? And if so, what—if anything—are the world's wealthiest and most powerful going to have to give up?

At Miraflores, there were various perspectives on the question of legitimate grievances. Of course, among those who strongly believe that terrorists are personally flawed, this question is not so important. Because if all terrorists are personally flawed, then only those personally flawed individuals have attacked in the past, and we can assume that will be more or less true in the future, regardless of whether their grievances are legitimate. By that line of reasoning, we might have a moral obligation to address grievances, but that would be, they think, separate from any benefit we might gain in terms of reducing or preventing terrorism. Prevention of terrorism, they might feel, is more likely to occur if we address the personal flaw of the terrorist, rather than the grievances the individual who may be flawed is attempting to bring to wider attention.

Could Terrorist Acts Ever Be Performed by Normal People?

There is a great deal of social science research detailing conditions under which normal people may be likely to act aggressively, though some would argue that the laboratory is so different from the real world that it is foolish to extrapolate. For example, ordinary people are more apt to act aggressively when told to do so by someone who seems to have an authority role, when they themselves are in a role that encourages or allows it, when they are in a uniform or their personal identity is otherwise subsumed to a group identity, and when the victim is distant, and has been depersonalized or dehumanized. All these conditions exist to varying degrees, as far as we know, for those who have been suicide terrorists, including the 9/11 terrorists (Zimbardo 2007). Indeed, under these conditions, it is the exception when someone steps forward to protest or refuse to engage in aggression. We might ask whether some of these conditions typically exist when a terrorist action takes place. An unanswered question, then, would be whether one could reduce terrorist actions by reducing these conditions.

What About Demographics and Motivation?

Several papers presented at the conference led conferees to wonder whether motivation to engage in terrorist acts, including suicide/martyr acts, varies by gender and age. There is some evidence—mostly case studies—that many adult female terrorists have been, prior to their actions, victims of sexual assault and gender-based oppression.[4] At least some of those women live in societies where it is likely that having been a victim of sexual assault would lead them to be rejected by their families and communities, leaving them almost no prospect for a normal life.

There is no comparable evidence with regard to males who become suicide/martyr terrorists, and while there are anecdotes about young girls (but not boys) who become suicide/martyr terrorists after being sexually assaulted, no systematic studies have so far been done, and thus we have no indication about whether this is a common pattern. Other motives described by girls, anecdotally, include opportunities for equality with their male peers, wanting to contribute to the cause (however perceived) that the group was fighting for, and adventure. However, the pattern with respect to adult females makes one wonder whether there are common factors contributing to becoming a suicide/martyr terrorist for girls, boys, and men. Alternatively, it is possible that sexual assault and rape are the most common ways that women have been silenced, abused, and traumatized, whereas men may have been silenced, abused, and traumatized more commonly in other ways—such as by nonsexual violence, alienation, or humiliation. Perhaps it is not specifically the sexual assault that leads to suicidal/martyrdom intent, but the effects of being mistreated and traumatized, in whatever form that may take. This leads us back to both the theories of personal flaw and the theories of legitimate grievances. Shall we interpret engagement in terrorist action after being silenced, abused, mistreated, and traumatized to be the result of a personal flaw or as the result of a legitimate grievance? What about when one perceives one's identity group, or one's offspring, as having been mistreated, abused, silenced, and traumatized? Is responding with violence a sign of personal flaw? Would it be more normal to respond with rededicated efforts to work within the system? Is working harder within the system a usual human response, or only likely for an unusually resilient, trusting individual? Can we define the conditions or personal traits that make it more likely what someone will do under pressure of being silenced and traumatized?

What About the Demographics of Child Terrorists?

Discussions of children who become terrorists at the conference did not turn to the topics many discussions at conferences in the United States do: Do children bear the same degree of guilt for their actions as adults? How could their family let this happen? Would they have been suicidal anyway, and was the conflict just a convenient way to kill themselves? People wonder how a child could be allowed to sign up for a terrorist action, and how family members could be proud of them for doing so. The intensity of concern and of emotions surrounding these discussions in many conferences arise chiefly because we tend to have our own families, neighborhoods, and communities as the prototype for family and for parent-child relationships. Few Americans with sufficient education and stature to be attending professional conferences have experienced the conditions of local war, or the disruption of parental caretaking efficacy that occurs when it is simply impossible to protect one's children's lives, much less see to it that they receive a good education. In addition, as noted before, American news media

tend to report on Palestinian children who engage in suicide/martyr actions in Israel, making it seem like a unique problem, when it is actually best understood as one type of situation in which children engage in terrorism, among many such situations in the world.

Comparing Child Terrorists with Child Soldiers

Ironically, while the actions of children who perform terrorist actions are apt to be blamed, by Americans, on the children and their parents, the actions of child soldiers who are part of rebel militias tend to be blamed on the adult soldiers who recruit them, use them for their own gains, and, often, mistreat them, and on the governments who are unable or unwilling to control those militias.

What About Distribution of Wealth and Resources?

Several social science disciplines study distribution of wealth and the effects of uneven access to resources. Wealth disparities are increasing rapidly around the world. Official numbers in the United States tell a stunning story. On December 15, 2007, the *NYTimes* reported, "The increase in incomes of the top 1 percent of Americans from 2003 to 2005 exceeded the total income of the poorest 20 percent of Americans, data in a new report by the *Congressional Budget Office shows.*"[5] It is part of standard courses of study in sociology, anthropology, political science, and economics. Curiously, few psychologists do. As a result no one discipline can be counted upon to look at the psychological effects of inequality. When they do, it is sometimes assumed that poor people have some mental health problem, such as low self-esteem, or mental illness, that inhibits them from becoming middle class. Indeed, psychologists in the United States tend to take middle class as normal or average, and expectable. So those conferees who talked about grievances would have a challenge if they tried to convince the researchers who believed that terrorism is a result of a personal flaw. While every one of the researchers would have told you that terrorism is most often the tactic of the less powerful side in a conflict, there is a great deal of work to be done considering how personal factors might interact with circumstances, if they do.

Several social scientists who were not at the conference, but whose ideas were discussed, make the following logic: Terrorist actions are rarely done alone, and when they are, they are not so deadly and not so worrisome. They are more like crime. Terrorism done in groups is more significant and more deadly—that is the "real" terrorism. And if someone in a group were mentally ill, the group would quickly drop them. In other words, terrorists acting in groups are not likely to be mentally impaired.

In short, the world's wealth is extremely unevenly divided, and the haves are more likely to be the victims of nonstate-sponsored terrorism. The haves, after

all, are more likely to be part of a large system, a state, and can afford a regular military. Indeed, the regular military may end up doing things that feel, to those attacked, a lot like terrorism, but the regular military is governed by rules of engagement, and so what feels like terrorism to the victims is considered by most to be collateral damage.

A Question That Did Not Come Up: Biological Determinism for Aggression

Freud thought human relationships were governed by two instincts: a positive instinct—to connect, love, support, etc. And a negative instinct—to fight, hate, aggress. This point of view has its proponents today as well. But it also has many opponents. Indeed, few psychologists see violent aggression or hatred as normal; most think it has to be explained. In 1983, the International Society for Research on Aggression, meeting in Seville, Spain, issued a statement about aggression. In short, the statement says that violence and aggression are not normal, expected, instinctive actions.

It appeared that the attendees at this conference were not proponents of the idea that terrorism and other forms of aggression are more normal. Although neither of the following views was represented at this conference, some evolutionary scientists believe that overpopulation inevitably leads to aggression. Still others believe that aggression is a universal human instinct. Of course if the first of those is true, the answer to terrorism may be reducing the birth rate—this, of course, assumes you could convince most—if not all—people to have fewer offspring. If the second is true—if aggression is an instinct—the answer might be stricter security or control, to deter expression of that instinct. Or it might be that social science research could be used to define circumstances that are less likely to bring out expression of that instinct. Furthermore, if aggression were to be found to be an instinct, an important question would be what sort of individual differences there are in degree of that instinct. Another important question would be how to define the circumstances most likely to trigger the instinct. For example, it is widely believed that the attachment instinct, that leads dependent individuals to form close bonds with their caregivers, is likely to be triggered when the individual is afraid or upset. In those instances, the caregiver is sought and is able to reduce the level of distress. If violence is an instinct, what are the conditions that elicit it. And how do those conditions relate to the conditions under which psychologically normal and healthy people are apt to act aggressively?

Mitigating the Impact of Terrorist Acts

Quite a lot of research has been done on how people reacted to the terrorist attacks of 9/11. A large amount of research done at first focused on how many

people reacted with high levels of distress, even with post-traumatic stress disorder, and how long those effects lasted. This seemed distasteful to some, since scientists were documenting, rather than ameliorating, their research participants' pain. Of course, generally accepted rules of research require that the scientists receive the consent of those they interview and study—informed consent. And those who oversee research, the Institutional Review Boards, are supposed to see that the research procedures make it likely that if anyone does not wish to participate, they will feel it is perfectly fine to decline. Still, studying victims and their families seems somehow less ethical, or perhaps more opportunistic, than research on preventing terrorism in the first place.

But mitigating the effects of terrorism is critical, since preventing it seems a long way off, and since, if the psychological, social, and economic impact is too great, it might destabilize a society. Furthermore, even the fear of future terrorism has the potential to cause radical changes in behavior. Not surprisingly, a great deal of research on this sort of topic has been done in Israel.

COGNITIVE DEVELOPMENT: THE BRILLIANT, EXASPERATING, DELIBERATE ADOLESCENT MIND

"We initially thought it was thunder and then the next thought was that it was a terrorist explosion," she said. "It sounded like strong thunder, but it kept going and going. It's nonstop. We can't see anything now."

"I thought it was a terrorist explosion or something because of everything that has been happening," he said.

—Two responses from a woman and a man working next door to the building where there was a steam pipe explosion on 42nd street in New York City on July 18, 2007, as quoted by Sewall Chan from the *New York Times*.

Twenty-First-Century Terrorism and the Development of Youthful Terrorists

Americans are paying a lot more attention to terrorism around the globe after the attacks of 2001. Furthermore, both scientific study and seemingly endless anecdotal accounts confirm that fear of future terrorism still affects the majority of American adults, even several years after September 11, 2001. This makes some sense given recent reports by those such as the NCTC (National Counter-Terrorism Center), which reported a 25 percent increase in attacks worldwide in 2006 as compared to 2005. However, it is interesting to note that of the fourteen-thousand attacks that were reported by the NCTC in 2006, 45 percent of these occurred in Iraq. The NCTC reports that for the Western hemisphere, attacks actually decreased by 15 percent. Europe and Eurasia saw a 15 percent decrease.

While the number of terrorist attacks overall is remaining fairly steady, or even decreasing, the number of such attacks where the terrorist planfully dies in the act

have grown exponentially over the last twenty-five years, according to terrorism expert Ariel Merari. We are here defining suicide or martyr terrorism attacks as those with the features described earlier: the planful and intentional act of killing oneself in the service of killing others; the victims including mostly—if not exclusively—civilians; the goals being to create fear and to achieve a political or ideological objective; and the action occurring outside the context of a traditional war between two recognized state entities. According to Ariel Merari (2007), there was one such attack in 1981, 6 in 1991, 61 in 2001, and 179 in 2004. Although the average age range of those committing these attacks has typically been about twenty-one to twenty-three years, a more recent and disturbing trend over the past decade has been the steady increase in youthful terrorists engaging in these acts. Americans are quite familiar with the concept of Palestinian teenagers who blow themselves up in Israel, but it is critical to note that such events are taking place in many parts of the world, and not all the perpetrators do so for the religion of Islam. As we write this, police have picked up a fifteen-year-old in Pakistan who claims to have been the next in line to kill himself and others in the service of assassinating Benazir Bhutto, had the attack on her earlier this month not been successful.[1]

Child Soldier, Child Terrorist

We believe that to understand children who engage in small or large acts of terrorism all around the globe, we have to look first at the problem of child soldiers, and only then at the problem of child terrorists. The understanding of adult terrorists helps us understand child terrorists only because, in most cases, adults recruit, train, and dispatch children to terrorist acts. We need to know about adult terrorists, especially those who recruit, train, and dispatch child terrorists, not because what we learn about why adults become terrorists also applies to children, but because we want to understand why and how they recruit children and we want to stop them. The line between child soldier and child terrorist is thin and permeable. We want to understand the process of recruitment to the cause, to the militia, and to the act of martyrdom.

Children and adolescents are easy targets for recruitment for several reasons, partly because of their perceived vulnerability to the influence of individuals seen as powerful and idealistic, things that reverberate with their own idealism and new sense of personal strength and status. That is, recruiters seeking to increase their forces may believe it will be easier to persuade and engage youthful candidates with slogans and promises than it is to engage adults, and it probably is. Of course, not all those children who are sent on suicide missions were recruited; some were kidnapped or threatened and forced to join militias, then given the special assignment of dying in an attack. And some who were kidnapped or forced to join find ways to leave. Some believe that even young orphans have

been kidnapped, raised, and trained for a suicide mission, and that few who were kidnapped at very young ages are able to escape.

Of course, besides being potentially easy to recruit, however, children are also easier to kidnap and coerce. And children are useful to the militia leaders—they can enter situations without inspiring fear, whereas adults might be suspected of being dangerous. In some missions, the very size of the child is useful, in that they may be able to get into and through places where an adult would simply not fit. Amnesty International reports that currently 250,000 children (defined as being under the age of 18) are participating in conflicts around the world, and an equal number more are ready to engage in conflict at any time. Although Amnesty reports that most youth who are actively participating in conflict are between the ages of 15 and 18, recruitment—or conscription by force—of youth into these organizations usually begins at about age 10, and sometimes younger. Wessells (2006, p. 47) reports that child soldiers were active in twenty-seven countries between 2001 and 2004, countries on several continents.

For those children who are recruited, or who seek out involvement in militias that engage in terrorism, the motivations are many and have been documented widely. Factors that have been considered include religious motivations (e.g., to achieve an afterlife in heaven for themselves and their loved ones or simply to do what they think is the will of god); a sense of injustice, humiliation, or revenge; financial or other gain for one's family; status; furthering of the political/ideological movement; a sense of grievances unaddressed, and of unfairness in distribution of power and wealth; and a genuine (if misguided) wish to help others through altruistic acts. First person accounts, including quotes from current or former terrorists, some of them young, are readily available. The reasons are varied and many. However, when considering this recent burgeoning of youth involvement in terrorist actions, we must consider: (1) the role of child and adolescent development, and how being young, seeing the world as a young person, and thinking like a young person, presents an array of vulnerabilities to becoming involved in violent activity, voluntarily or involuntarily; and (2) how the context in which one develops affects the fundamental capacities, as well as the content, of one's developing ability to think.

Development

Developmental science has historically focused on how individuals *evolve* over the life span, in many different areas. It is concerned with how people change in terms of their physical appearance (physical development), the way they reason and form judgments (intellectual/cognitive development), the way they experience and express emotions (emotional development), and the way they understand themselves and others in social contexts (social development). All of these areas of development are dependent on brain development. Further, all these

experiences *affect* brain development. That is, it is not a one-way street, with brain development driving experience, choices, and actions. Experiences, choices, and actions also affect the development of the brain. A great deal of work has been done showing that trauma, if not addressed properly, adversely impacts not only the child's emotions, but their cognitive processes, and the development of their brains. Timely intervention can prevent these changes, but there is, as yet, not enough research to know how to effectively intervene when trauma is likely to be repeated or continue, in the future.

Particularly during adolescence (which we are defining to include ages from 10 to 18), there is rapid change and transition in social, cognitive, and emotional development, a tendency for behaviors and choices to become patterns, and for the patterns to become well-established. While all these areas of development play a role in the child's vulnerability to joining a terrorist group, the cognitive and social areas seem, from the research we have reviewed, to be the most important to consider, and both have to be considered in the context of the environment in which the children grow up.

Cognitive Development and Youth in War-Affected Areas

Perhaps one of the most famous psychologists to study cognitive development, Jean Piaget, developed a theory for how all people evolve in terms of the way they think and reason. Over several decades of research across cultures, this theory has proved useful as a way to think about the development of cognitive abilities, with context considered, suggesting that there are neurological changes associated with the behavioral and cognitive changes Piaget observed. We make use of the theory here, together with more modern research findings, to begin to explain how it is that a child in a war zone can develop the capacity to kill himself and others, and how a child can come to understand such a choice as a heroic, prosocial act, helping the community. In order to do so, we call on Western theory and cross-cultural research, and we illustrate with our experiences in Sri Lanka.

Beginning at the first *sensorimotor* stage in infancy, the baby's focus is on coordinating sensory perceptions and simple motor behaviors. The youngest baby learns quickly that certain actions can create certain effects—biting a toy that squeaks or jumping in a baby seat. At first, these effects are created by chance and the learning is by association. The child happens to pushdown on a squeaky toy and it makes a noise. She repeats the action to find the same effect, etc. Moving through this stage, children begin to understand a world outside of them and begin to interact with it in deliberate ways. Of note, children fully develop a sense of *object permanence* only toward the end of infancy, when they consistently understand that even when an object—or a person—is taken away and placed out of sight, it continues to exist and can be refound. Rabain-Jamin (1994) has shown that even at this infancy period, parents in cultures that focus on group

identity and the collective good talk to their infants differently than those in cultures that focus on the individual. This early talk previews a whole set of spoken and unspoken lessons about empathy, altruism, loyalty to the group, and the critical importance of group identity, cohesion, and harmony.

Guided participation, as Rogoff, Mistry, Goncu, and Mosier (1993) define it, is the development and socialization of children "through active participation in cultural systems of practice in which children, together with their caregivers and other companions, learn and extend skills, values, and knowledge of their community" (p. 1). The consequences of these varying styles across different cultures leads to different constructions of *self* that are contingent upon the mores which shape them. Kagitcibasi (1996, p. 53) speaks to this when she says, "The concept of self is variously understood in different cultural contexts," where differing customs and traditions drive the process of *guided participation* in distinct ways. These distinctions are then naturally rooted in notions of self within each child, reflecting the virtues of the culture.

Cognitive development continues, of course, all through infancy and the early toddler period, with elaborations and applications of ways of thinking. Babies are learning, for example, to compare objects to an internal image of what the object should look like and to notice deficient or broken objects. In the United States, young toddlers may be seen holding up objects with missing or defective parts, saying "broken." They are also beginning to develop an early sense of identity, being capable of recognizing themselves in a mirror, for example. In the United States, parents often joke about the emergence of the term and concept of "me" as in "me do it myself." Children may also call themselves by their names, with a child named Bobby saying, for example, "Bobby do it!" There is an important divergence of lessons that begin here, taught by parents, other family members, and members of the community: How important is individual identity? This early divergence prefigures dramatic differences in how adolescents from individually oriented cultures, as compared with those from collectively oriented cultures, view themselves.

Early cross-cultural research found that adolescents from collective cultures, when asked to talk about a sense of self, had a hard time doing so. They simply did not think of themselves as having importance as individuals apart from the group they belonged to—something we who grew up in an individually oriented culture can barely understand—and had not been trained to consider their own identities and needs separately from those of the group.[2]

In our research in Sri Lanka, we asked adolescents a question that we were assured teenagers in the United States and the EU answered readily. We said we were interested in decision-making and asked for an instance where the child had been faced with a decision where they did not know what was the right decision or what was the wrong decision to make. Despite the assurances we had had that children in the United States and EU found this a very good question and were

able to talk about both concrete and abstract dilemmas about values, virtually none of the children we interviewed answered. (At first, we thought perhaps it was not being translated correctly, but after a small number of older children did answer, we concluded that the problem was not with faulty translation.) Our translator and cultural consultant explained that in Sri Lanka, children knew the right thing to do, because their families had taught them when they were small. When we asked her what about if it were a new situation—one that the children's parents had not thought of, she said they would then ask an older person to help them make a decision. But, we said, what if it was an emergency and there was no time to ask? She said that in an emergency, they would call for help and a whole bunch of people would come and together solve the problem. This was a stunning and dramatic explanation of the fundamental difference in the individual versus collective way of thinking. As this sunk in, we asked one last question of the translator. We used an example from one of our colleagues, James Day, who does research on religion and moral development in the EU. He said that a teenager might, when initially asked for such a dilemma, talk about a dilemma from everyday life, such as being asked by a friend whether you liked her dress, not liking it, and having to decide between telling the truth and hurting her feelings, on the one hand, or making her feel good but not being completely honest on the other (Day, pers. comm., April 2007). The translator was very sure that the correct answer to this, as taught to children in Sri Lanka, would be to tell her you like the dress, since peoples' feelings are so important. Values that include harmony are common in collective cultures, and this, it seemed to us, is a good example.

A few days later, a small problem came up that perfectly exemplified the translator's explanation of how an emergency would be dealt with. Someone had locked her key in her room and needed to get in. In this case, she did not even have to ask for help. Someone saw her trying to open the window. First one, then within a very few minutes six or seven friends and acquaintances were there to help. Two of the people who came to help were able to cooperate to get the window open enough to reach in and unlock the door.

As we told this story of the translator's explanation to various people who were aware of the difference between individual-oriented and collective-oriented societies, we heard other examples. One that seemed a helpful illustration of the difference between the two types of societies was provided by someone who had tried to explain the problem of homelessness to a person who had lived his whole life in a Latin American country. The Latin American man was puzzled to the point of near-disbelief. He asked many questions, such as, "Are there not enough homes to go around?" and "Don't they have any family?" It was simply unthinkable to him that there could be enough homes and yet someone would be left to live on the streets.

We add these examples because most of the places in the world where there are child soldiers and where children become engaged in terrorism, including actions

in which they planfully die, are more collective-oriented than individual-oriented societies. Even those youthful terrorists who have grown-up in Europe tend to be closely connected with societies or communities with collective values, whether these are the country of origin of close family members or closely knit minority groups that foster fierce loyalty. Indeed as McCauley and others have pointed out, terrorist organizations themselves foster values that are associated with collective societies, including loyalty to the group and holding the group's welfare above one's personal welfare. For some examples, the London subway bombing was done by citizens with close ties to, and who identified with, a collective culture. Japan, where the Aum Shinryiko sect engaged in terrorism, is a society that includes elements of both collective and individual societies. The sect clearly fostered collective values, at least in regard to the sect itself, if not the country as a whole.

One of the core differences between collective and individual societies that is not often talked about is loyalty. In individual-oriented societies, people are expected to choose the groups with which they identify, to which they show loyalty, and to remain with those groups only as long as they wish. Critical to our understanding of children who engage in terrorism, collectively oriented societies tend to expect lifelong loyalty to the family, community, and ethnic group into which one is born. An anecdotal illustration of this comes from the fictional account of Carmen, in the novel *Bel Canto*. At one point, she is asked by the hostages to do a favor that would enable two of the hostages who have fallen in love to be together, violating the generals' rules. Carmen, a youthful soldier/terrorist, struggles with this because it speaks to her of loyalty. In her thinking, if she helps the hostages, it fundamentally changes her identity as part of the militia group, and challenges her loyalty to the people for whom she is fighting. The hostage who asks her for this favor, by contrast, has no idea at all of how much it means to her, thinking of it as a simple favor.

The next major transition in thinking is called the transition to the preoperational stage or change, just beginning roughly at the age of 2. At this stage, new capacities to speak and understand another person's point of view are emerging, but they are limited and the conclusions drawn by the child about others' perceptions and thoughts are often just plain wrong. This kind of thought process is known as *egocentricity*, or the notion that everyone (and even inanimate objects, such as dolls) experiences the world as they do. A child talking on the phone with someone thousands of miles away may talk about what he sees, as if the person at the other end must of course see the same things—and this is without video phones or computer cameras. She might say, for example, "Grandma, look at what Spot is doing now" (referring to the family dog, which Grandma cannot see). Thinking is also precausal. That is, although children are sometimes able to systematically reason through situations, the conclusions are often inconsistent with fact. Coincidences of timing may suffice to cause the child to assume causality. For example, a child may believe that her father brushing his teeth causes the

tap water to turn on. Because of the child's limited life experiences, appearances dominate over informed, considered, logical thought. This is not so surprising, since, after all, the child's world is full of surprising new knowledge, and awakenings. Father's shaving might just as well turn on the water as the remote turns on the television or opens the garage door. Children in a war zone at this age will have little accurate knowledge of why there are soldiers or police, or why people disappear. If, as often happens with the best intentions, adults try to keep the child cheerful and shielded from the true horrors of war, the child may be left to draw his or her own conclusions, very likely faulty ones. Gradually, life experiences and observations enable the child to make better predictions and explanations, paving the way for the next transition.

Logical reasoning—at least the beginnings of it—emerges at the *concrete operational* stage at roughly age 7 to 8, the beginning of the next major transition in thought capacity. Here, children are less distracted by visual arrays and qualities, and beginning to focus on concepts. They are able to mentally order and classify objects into groups based correctly on the thing's unchanging identity, such as fruits versus vegetables, whereas earlier they might have begun to categorize things that way, but gotten distracted by the colors or shapes so that each group the child made might have two or three rationales. The child might start out with a red apple and an orange in one group and a green pepper and yellow bean in another. However, when they next had to categorize a red pepper, they might just as well put it with the red apple as with the green pepper. In a war zone, children who might have categorized everyone carrying a rifle together in a category like "big people with rifles," but once they reach the age of concrete operations, they might begin to separate the categories by allegiance—members one fighting group being in a different category from those in a different fighting group.

At this new stage, children also realize that certain properties of an object will remain the same even when other superficial characteristics are altered. This is referred to as the principle of *conservation*. The classic example of this is when a tall and narrow glass of water is poured into short and wide glass. Prior to achieving this stage, most children would believe that, because the line of water is not as high it must contain less water. However, those having achieved the concrete stage would be able to understand that the amounts are the same, despite the appearance having changed, knowing that pouring does not affect amount. The child also understands that one action will reverse another action, such as pouring the liquid back in the glass. This is referred to as the law of *reversibility.* Being able to mentally imagine reversing an action, for example, means that the child can realize that liquid poured from one glass to another can be poured back (and would look the same). Such thinking is carried out in the presence of objects, however. Thinking at this stage is categorical and finite, and problems are conceived of as having definitive and specific solutions. Truth is also conceptualized as categorical and thus universal. In a war-affected area, this might be the

level of reasoning engaged in when, tribe, ethnicity, race, or religion is conceptualized categorically into right versus wrong, or believer versus heretic, us versus them. It would be quite tempting to militias to recruit or kidnap children at this thought level, because they would be amenable to a strong belief in the rightness of the cause, the people, and the religion. And quite amenable to thinking that the others are simply wrong. This is an age and stage of clarity in judgment—which is, in a complex world, a limiting world view.

Only at the final *formal operational* stage does abstract, logical, hypothetical, and syllogistic reasoning, reasoning of the type that begins "If A is stronger than B and B is stronger than C, then..." emerge. For children who have had some formal education, the capacity for this way of thinking emerges at roughly age 11 to 12. Here, the young adolescent begins to develop the ability to think hypothetically, and understand that there may be multiple ways of solving a particular problem, although one way is apt to be better than others. Problem solving is methodical and involves forming and testing hypotheses about the world, something referred to as *hypotheticodeductive* reasoning. Interestingly, there have been multiple studies that have indicated that many adults never reach formal operational thinking, and remain at the concrete operational stage, at least in some domains. Use of concrete, rather than formal thinking processes in a variety of areas has consequences that, while often undesirable for the individual, and for society as a whole, can be simpler and easier in some situations and may even be preferable in some areas.

What is important for our understanding of terrorism, however, is that leaders find their followers more malleable if the followers do not think in formal terms. Formal thinkers in a given domain may want evidence and logic from their leaders. They may critically assess what the leaders say, using logic and evidence of their own. Leaders are less likely to be able to use charisma, slogans, and emotional bonding to keep their followers in control if the followers think in formal terms in the area in which they are leading them. The fact that both Nazi Germany and Aum Shinrikyo (Japan's terrorist group) included trained physicians helps us to illustrate an important point about areas of thinking.

Clearly, in order to attain a medical degree, these individuals had to be competent at thinking logically in the area of science. Yet in the domain of patriotism (Germany) or religion (Japan), the physicians were not thinking logically, but were under the sway of charismatic leaders and of group belief systems or group think. These examples illustrate the concept called domain specificity in development. An individual might well have attained formal operational thought in one domain (engineering, science) but may not use that advanced level thought in other domains (patriotism, religion) or when group decision-making and group loyalty prevail.

In 1986, just before the disastrous launch of the *Challenger* spacecraft, the vice-president and director for engineering of the subcontractor responsible for

the O-rings in the *Challenger* was specifically asked "to take off his engineering hat and put on his management hat" according to testimony heard by the presidential commission on the Space Shuttle disaster. (Report of the Presidential Commission on the Space Shuttle disaster, chapter 5.) The engineers, according to that testimony, were not in favor or launching the spacecraft due to the cold temperatures predicted at launch time, and their concern about the likely performance of the O-rings at those temperatures. This is a rather stunning example of someone being asked to switch domains so that a lower level of thought and decision-making could prevail. In switching hats, the engineer appears to have used a lower level of cognitive processing, subject to pressures involving politics, and disfavoring logical and procedural thought. We have concluded from our research on terrorist leaders that they either are taking off their formal operational "hat" or at least asking their followers to do so.

Another recruitment method used with people whose grasp on formal thought may be a bit shaky is to provide them incorrect or selected data on which to practice their capacity. For example, a terrorist recruiter may tell a child who is newly able to engage in syllogistic reasoning something like the following: They (the opposition) are harming our people. The militia is the only way to stop them. You can help stop the harm by joining the militia. If you and your friends do not join, there will be no militia, and if there is no militia, the opposition will destroy our people. This is a very clear logical thought process, except that it is based on flawed statements. It is as if you were told, "There is a group of people starving on the other side of the highway. The only way to solve the problem is for the highway to close. Only you and your friends can close down the highway by marching across it. If you do not march across the highway, the people will starve." A child newly capable of syllogistic reasoning may find this appealing. The seasoned thinker will ask about the truth of the statements that form the structure for the logical process.

Central to this concept of formal operational thinking, young adolescents shift in terms of their thinking and begin to tackle very abstract issues, notably identity and "who am I?" In his theory of psychosocial development, Erik Erikson expounded on this and talked about how for young adolescents, this time marks the beginning self-exploration, and how past experiences and future goals give rise to a general sense of self. Choices are made regarding occupation, sexual orientation, religious identity, and political identity—all as components of what we stand for in life. The challenge is to explore these issues and eventually make commitments. Not having an identity is not an option, and the process of choosing one is difficult. In many parts of the world where youth are engaged in fighting, identities are predefined by the community, there is less choice and less burden to choose, and the struggle to form an identity, though potentially challenging, is different from the struggle to find an identity in an individually oriented culture.

Group-Defined Identity

However, even in the United States, group-defined identities play a role in adolescent development, although the groups doing the defining include groups of choice, as well as groups into which one was born. Harvard Professor and Psychologist Robert Kegan discussed this issue of identity formation in youth, and using mostly examples from individually oriented cultures still concluded that youth almost invariably define "self" in terms of the social institutions to which they belong. Social groups essentially become the framework used for understanding the basic identity question: Who am I? Answers include: I am an athlete on the baseball team, a musician in the band, an academic competing on the math team, the president of the Civics Club. (Not, note, I am the son of so and so, a member of this ethnic group, a resident of this town.) The social group is what leads to a sense of identity—even if, in the United States, the social group is a chosen group, joined more or less voluntarily. Still, without it, confusion and even crisis result. In some parts of the world, terrorist organizations take advantage of this need to belong, and represent social institutions that both affirm the identities into which the child was born and, for many young people, provide a very powerful source for expanding that identity. Martyrs are seen as superstars, as icons of the movement, and as heroes of the groups into which they were born. Serving in this role then adds a new dimension to self, one that is potent and influential. In the context of the perceived wrongs that are being perpetrated against the youth's people and against the movement, assuming this role provides for an authoritative counterforce.

Deciding to Engage in a Terrorist Act: The Youthful Brain

And what rational and psychological skills do adolescents bring the decision of whether to engage in a terrorist act? The answer is an incompletely developed decision-making apparatus that will not be complete till age 25 or so. Psychologists believe that the human brain is not designed to assess and make decisions about the risks and threats of the modern world. Add to this the challenges of making such decisions with an apparatus that affords adolescents a solid ability to analyze pros and cons, but a very strong bias toward pros, toward near term rewards, and toward risk-taking.

The bias toward risk-taking may be a result of not yet having developed intuitive or gist reactions to events—the kind of quick analysis that Gladwell was talking about in the popular book *Blink*. Explanation in Baird, et al., *The Teen Brain*. Adults might have a stronger emotional intuitive negative reaction toward engaging in terrorist activity. (Is it a good idea to blow yourself up in order to blow others up? Or, in our earlier example, is it a good idea to march across a highway? Most adults are likely to have a strong reaction that leads them to avoid such a choice.) Indeed, in some situations, adult risk analysis may be weighted a little

too heavily on avoidance of low incidence, disastrous outcomes as a result of this gist thinking, such as having a gist reaction that they would rather travel 400 miles in a car rather than take a plane, out of fear of a plane crash. This is a poor decision in terms of systematic risk analysis, yet some adults choose not to fly, no matter how clear the analysis is, because of the strong risk aversion bias against low incidence disasters. Adolescents do not yet have this gist capacity well-developed. As you will see, in some instances, this may even give adolescents an advantage in decision-making, but it sometimes disadvantages them.

Furthermore, adolescents are biased against looking at long-term eventualities. We know they would not have an easy time getting out of a terrorist organization (or a violent gang) if they join, but they do not think about that problem, because their minds simply do not process future risk well, and they tend to choose near-term gain or pleasure, even if it comes with long-term risk, more so than adults. Some risks may be less worrisome than others. Getting a radical haircut or risking a small amount of money, for example, or choosing to play football, while not without serious potential consequence, are risks we more or less accept as normal for adolescents. Even driving a bit fast or trying out a motorcycle. These are things we know bring some risks, but a degree of risk that most parents accept, even if reluctantly, are not unusual parts of growing up. For other parents in the world, however, the risk analyses made by their teenagers weigh out differently. Thus the risks taken by a teenager who lives in the South Bronx, or South Central LA, or in countless other parts of the United States where gang culture rules, must make their way through life assessing the risks of, say, walking to school one way versus another, or taking this bus versus that. In war-affected areas, teenagers also face risks on a daily basis, and they are not consistently in control of the risks they take.

The Ecology of Development

All development, of course, occurs within context. That is, although some aspects of development seem to be consistent across various neighborhoods and cultures, the context matters both in terms of kinds of things that are going on and in terms of adolescents' increasing ability to handle these things as they develop. It is useful to think about the developmental process in images of concentric circles—some use the metaphor of the onion; others of tree rings—where each layer represents a set of forces acting on the individual and shaping their evolution. The late Dr. Urie Bronfenbrenner developed the bioecological systems theory to describe this complex set of relationships, where at the center of the onion or tree trunk are the biological and genetic systems that provide the blueprints for growth and maturation. As the person grows, people, events, and environmental factors shape the ongoing processes from the outside in, while the growing person also exerts some influence outward, on the environment. Take for example, as parents know, the difference between a household with a quiet,

self-contained child versus one who is energetic and rambunctious. Indeed from infancy on, households differ according to the temperament of their infants. How much sleep do parents get? How much does the child need to be entertained? How hard is it to keep the child engaged, quiet, and also safe? How hard to keep the child from disrupting things in a store or on a bus? Parents have to act differently with each child, trying to draw out the quiet child, or to channel the energy of the more rambunctious one. And of course that is just one dimension. There are children who are athletically gifted and those who are not; some are academically talented, others not at all inclined that way. Some have many friends and activities; others have few. The parents, the school, the community all adjust and also encourage the child to moderate their temperaments as well.

After the child's own core temperament and biological processes of development, the next ring or layer is the family and immediate social environment that exerts substantial influence in shaping the individual, and, as noted earlier, is shaped by the individual as well. Family here might mean extended family or chosen kin. It might include godparents, aunts, uncles, great grandparents, nieces, and so on—in some cultures, an entire village serves as close family, with a variety of adults providing basic care to the child. This level, consisting of the closely connected group, is followed by the larger neighborhood, community, state, nation, geographic region, and ultimately the world. For most children in the world, the relationship with the neighborhood, community, and world, is not totally mediated by their parents. That is, they have close relationships with family, but they have other relationships with other children and members of their communities—relationships that are direct, and do not depend on the parents being intermediaries. In those contexts, too, they are actively assessing risks, and they bring intimate knowledge of the risks, as well as a less than perfectly developed ability to decide how to deal with them.

In a book called *Fist, Stick, Knife, Gun,* the well-known and highly regarded Geoffrey Canada, president and CEO of the Harlem Children's Zone, an activist engaged in work for children and adolescents in New York City, and who himself grew up in the South Bronx at a time when guns were less prevalent than other weapons, writes about children influenced by the neighborhood group, and who keep secrets from their parents. He does not condemn children for keeping secrets, because they know things that their parents would not understand. Like Rosen in his analysis of child soldiers, Canada's statements suggest that some children are facing real danger, and that adults should respond to the real dangers. Like Rosen, he sees children as sometimes facing survival issues, and adults as sometimes acting as if the engagement in conflict were the problem, rather than the children's attempt to solve the problems they face.

There are children all over this country who are hiding weapons in their closets, in sneaker boxes under their beds, under their sweaters in their dresser

drawers. They are certain that they need their guns or knives for their own safety, sure that their very lives depend on having those weapons. We will never convince them to give up their weapons with fancy television jingles or with marches alone. What these children need is a sense of safety, a certainty of surviving as they go to school or to the store (Canada 1995, p. 75).

And what country is he talking about? The United States. The year? 1995. Our experiences providing services in a juvenile court clinic near Boston from 2003 to 2007, convinced us that things in the United States are not better in respect to fear and danger for children in poor and violent communities now than they were in 1995. Children in the United States have lives that are secret from their parents; they respond directly to conditions in their communities, and so do children in war zones. Children in war-affected areas may also have lives that are, if not secret, at least not openly shared, with their parents. They learn things from other kids and from respected adults with whom their parents may not be well-acquainted. This might include clergy and it might include members of a militia.

Even before globalization, children around the world shared a culture to some extent. That is, children in many parts of the world had access to TV, to the occasional movie, to newspapers and magazines, even if they were out of date, and to stories of people who had visited more developed countries—stories that were listened too attentively by youth. Cell phone and Internet technology have brought many more of the world's youth much more news and information about the rest of the world. Thus the influence on children of places and people they have never even met has increased over time. Within each of these domains—then—family, community, region, and world—youth are influenced and youth influence the areas as well. To some degree, these influences are filtered through their parents, but not completely. Not only are there unique individual, familial, community, cultural, and systemic influences that act upon and shape the individual, but also each child has a unique set of influences. And those influences also influence each other. That is, the child's family influences the community, as well as the community influencing the child and family. The reasons why children may choose to blow themselves and others up are many and complex. Anyone wishing to understand the influences on any one child who becomes engaged in terrorism will have to think in very complex terms. There is, for each child, a dynamic, interactive system of mutual influences. We are most interested in finding what commonalities exist. What is similar about the bioecological systems of children around the world who engage in terrorist actions.

The Propensity to Engage in Terrorist Acts

Recently, Fathali Moghaddam proposed a framework for understanding how people move along a path which results in committing a terrorist act, with

specific focus on the underlying psychological and social processes contributing to this evolution. Using the "staircase" metaphor, Moghaddam illustrates how an individual progresses to a point where destruction of one's perceived enemy is the only solution that is acceptable, even if this means the destruction of one's self. When considering the steady increase in youth committing terrorist acts over the past decade, the issue of development becomes central to this thesis.

At the ground floor, Moghaddam highlights *perceived deprivation* as being a critical variable setting someone along this path. As Moghaddam points out, such perception may come about for many reasons, including economic and political hardships, as well as perceived insults to one's individual or group identity. Based on these insults, an individual usually takes one of two paths: (1) continuing to live their lives as is, despite the surrounding conditions not being ideal; or (2) challenge these systems and rise up to change them. However, it is important to note that it is this sense of basic sense of individual and collective deprivation (constituting a "grievance") that is the foundation for future escalation.

Moghaddam points out that in the case of modern Islamic terrorism, the perceived deprivation or insult is against an identity that is rooted radical interpretations of religion. For religious fundamentalists, religion serves as the most basic vehicle through which its following derives a sense of identity. Therefore, when this collective identity is threatened, either through increasing secularization, westernization, or U.S. troops setting foot on the soil of the holy Islamic sites, the response becomes immediately clear: retaliate as a way to maintain dignity and strength in the face of such assault. Young people are targeted in mosques throughout the Islamic world, and they are vulnerable to such targeting because: (1) they are striving for identity rooted in the culture around them, and finding identity in faith; and (2) they are more prone to the categorical, lower level, thinking that is requisite for someone to move through the staircase and ultimately commit a terrorist act.

On the first and second floors of the staircase, terrorist organizations ferment a process of solidifying in-group and out-group dynamics, and polarizing the identities of the two. Some who have made it to these floors will understand that there are alternative ways to affect change, and many will seek nonviolent routes and not travel up the staircase. Others, including many of the group's youth, will continue down this path of dichotomizing the participants into an "us versus them" dynamic. Youth are particularly vulnerable to this process because of their incomplete neurological and cognitive development. Youth are also vulnerable because of their striving for identity, and what better place to find it in a revolution? And youth are vulnerable because of their approach to risk assessment, valuing short-term gain, paying less attention to long-term cost, and not engaging in the gist (or "gut") reaction that might lead many an adult to say—"Blow myself up? Bad idea!"

At the third floor, recruits have been identified and youth are further indoctrinated as to the ideals of the terrorist organization. According to Moghaddam,

they usually begin living secret, dual lives, and further embed themselves with the organization and cause. They are not, of course, as we noted earlier, the first or only youth to have secret lives. On the fourth floor, this process continues although the youth is usually being lined up for the martyrdom operation. Youth are further isolated from outside influences and other competing perspectives, and their categorical, "us versus them" point of view becomes increasingly entrenched—this is the premeditated plan of their trainers and dispatchers: they are deliberately so indoctrinated. This occurs to the point that the terrorist organization in general, and the specific mission ahead, becomes seen as the only solution to the overarching problem. Moghaddam points out that another very important thing that occurs at this stage is that the youth are treated like celebrities by their superiors, and are held high in the eyes of the organization. In doing this, they cement the identities of these young people and fill an otherwise empty void. In addition, however, they touch on a typical adolescent thought distortion: the belief that one is important and being observed by others. We see this in the United States where our teenaged sons and daughters spend hours on one or two details of their appearance, and when they are so painfully self-conscious. The incorrect belief is that others will notice every detail about them, for example. This very adolescent trait is again used and abused by the trainers and dispatchers—those who are preparing to send the adolescents to an untimely death.

At the fifth and final stages, the act is committed. It is justified in terms of the extreme categorization of us versus them that has embedded, where innocent civilians are now seen as part of the enemy because they support the government in some way, or because they fail in some test of extreme faith or goodness. Moghaddam argues that this causes a great psychological distance between the perpetrator and victim, and allows the act to be committed on a greater, more idealistic level, as opposed to a simple murdering of an innocent person. Social psychologists would understand this in terms of the importance of dehumanizing the enemy in order to maximize the chances that the adolescent will be able to act violently toward that enemy.

Ironically, this process of moving through the staircase is developmental in nature, but it is the very opposite of the positive developmental models that most psychologists build. It begins with a perceived deprivation that is the spark. This spark is then fanned by a larger organization with specific goals for violence. People move through this staircase differently, with some never entering at all, and others moving to a middle floor and then deciding on different courses of action or strategies for negotiating the problem. Others move all the way through, and slowly narrow their perspective on the dilemma before them. More and more, the enemy is perceived as being in direct contrast to the in-group and organization, and presenting a mortal threat. The narrowing of viewpoints is the exact opposite of what developmentally oriented education is supposed to accomplish. The children caught in this staircase are being systematically

subjected to the undoing of cognitive developmental achievements. More and more, the terrorist organization is seen as the only choice for a solution, and the lens narrows further until the individual reaches the top of the staircase and understands the mission as the only way out.

Youth are particularly vulnerable to this process because of inherent developmental factors that preclude them from being able to understand these dynamics differently. They are less able to see the dilemmas before them in complex terms to be solved using a myriad of other alternatives. The categorical thinking that is propagated by terrorist organizations naturally attaches itself to the adolescent, because this is the lens through which the world has been seen, and where the adolescent may still be most comfortable. More than this, the issue of identity and meaning associated with being a part of a terrorist organization is also a powerful force guiding this process. At a point where young people are working very hard to negotiate their own sense of self, the terrorist organization intercedes and provides a very clear, simple, and powerful answer. This is reinforced by the sense of acclaim and celebrity they experience, and makes it even more difficult to entertain other possible paths. The only path, then, for some adolescents is the one up the staircase. (Perhaps a staircase down, into a hellish death, might be a more apt analogy.)

The Production Line Analogy

Ariel Merari puts forth a similar paradigm for how people, and particularly young people, come to engage in suicide/martyrdom terrorism. He uses the *production line* analogy, and emphasizes the role of the collective group in cultivating and influencing the eventual martyr. The ultimate act is as much about the inherent agreement between the organization and the individual as it is about the political and social meaning associated with it. In his study of Palestinian martyrdom terrorists, Merari discusses three components to this process.

The first facet is one of indoctrinating the soon to be martyr by the senior members of the organization. Building upon the motivational foundation that is already present, this process involves reinforcing the ideals and righteousness of the movement and solidifying further the commitment of the recruit. In the context of radical religious organizations, religion is used as the glue to cement fidelity. The conflict is portrayed as one of protecting religion against the aggressor at all costs, and the organization is construed as the vehicle for resistance. Martyrdom operations are understood as being honorable and moral ways of serving the religious institution, protecting it from this perceived aggression, and ensuring one's seat in the afterlife.

Building on the first, the second aspect of this process involves the organization cementing the individual's commitment to the task by slowly closing the exit doors around the person. This is analogous to Moghaddam's *staircase* analogy

discussed earlier, where as the soon-to-be martyr ascends the stairs, fewer and fewer choices are available to them. They become more and more cornered. Merari talks about how using videotaped farewell messages and referring to these individuals as "living martyrs" backs these people into a corner where the thought of breaking commitment to the task becomes more and more abhorrent.

The final aspect to Merari's model focuses on the role of public support and "normalizing" this process in the eyes of both the martyr and the general public. This process involves embedding this within the culture of the society through songs, videos, and is even encouraged in children's play. As these norms embed deeper and deeper into the zeitgeist of the society, the taboo around it plummets. The actions come to be sanctioned by the general public as a means of resisting and combating the aggressor. Most notably, this strategy is also reinforced by the simple fact that it is highly successful. During the second intifada, support for the use of terrorist tactics by the Palestinians against the Israelis rose as high as 85 percent. The success of these tactics hinges on the fact that it is difficult to predict or prevent, and it usually results in a high body count. In some cases, such as the train bombings against Madrid in 2004, it also leads to major policy changes by the corresponding government. The sense of mastery and power that results from this can be intoxicating for the young person signing up to be the next martyr.

Woven throughout this framework, Merari speaks to developmental factors including identity, context, and power in his analysis of Palestinian martyrdom terrorists. The factors associated with this climb to blowing one's self up serve a dual purpose: (1) they fuel a sense of identity and purpose within young people, who otherwise may be struggling to find this; and (2) they slowly close other doors of alternative courses of action, and commit the individual to the task ahead. Young people are particularly vulnerable to this process because, developmentally speaking, they are at a point in their lives where identity and a sense of purpose are primary and they are more prone to look toward authority figures to provide this sense of direction to them.

Merari also speaks to this when he discusses the many young martyrs who had left notes behind after committing the act. Rather than projecting a sense of hopelessness and despair, these young people conceptualized the attack as an act of power and control, a way of manipulating an aggressor that is perceived as omnipotent. It was conceived of as being for the greater good of the ideal, and was executed from a position of strength. The "identity crisis" then as proposed by Erikson had been solved. The youth had become martyrs willing to sacrifice themselves for the organization and revel in the benefits of the afterlife.

Preventing the Recruitment of Youth as Martyrs

In a timely 2006 article appearing in the journal, *Psychological Science,* Arie Kruglanski and Shira Fishman detail how terrorism is propagated and reinforced

as the tactic of choice within certain societies. In paraphrased form, it: (1) is a means to achieve the ends; (2) more effective than other tactics; and (3) does not conflict with existing societal mores. Given these principles, they conclude that to effectively counter this problematic trend, several conditions must be met: (1) it must be shown that these methods are not effective; (2) there are other, better alternatives to achieve the desired ends; and (3) it conflicts inherently with the principles of the society. In his 2006 *Science* article, Scott Atran put this even more succinctly:

> A first line of defense is to get the communities from which suicide attackers stem to stop the attacks by learning how to minimize the receptivity of mostly ordinary people to recruiting organizations (p. 1534).

Addressing this problem for all people is complex, and involves consideration of many different variables. However, as Merari has pointed out, there is a significant subcurrent to this phenomenon where young people are targeted as recruits for reasons that include being unattached and more susceptible to the influence of the organization for identity formation and cohesion of self/group.

With respect to the issue of youth involvement, several specific issues must be considered. First, the underlying society must acknowledge how powerful terrorist organizations are in providing a sense of identity to young people, and how some youth are inherently driven to this kind of activity for purposes of self-definition. There is an obvious and inherent synergy between the two, with both having their needs met by the other despite different underlying motivations. Similar to the phenomenon of gangs within the United States, there are multiple levels of infrastructure that must be considered in combating this problem. Focus should be paid to the individual, family, community, society, and country, because as Bronfenbrenner has showed us, there are powerful forces shaping the person at each level.

Second, because of underlying developmental vulnerabilities, young people are more prone to submit to those seen as the authority. Those in senior more authoritative positions are looked to as the holders of truth and knowledge. Therefore, they must be obeyed because theirs is the righteous path. Because of their underlying cognitive abilities and simplicity in understanding these very complex issues, there is less ability to understand that different, alternative approaches to addressing these problems exist, let alone the capacity to evaluate these approaches systematically. They are rather more likely to look to those senior to them for the single answer to the dilemma because they do not yet have the cognitive infrastructure to think about these issues in different, more complex ways.

Third, as Kegan and others have taught us, social groups are extraordinarily powerful forces in the lives of the adolescent. Terrorist groups, similar to their

gang counterparts within the United States, provide for a sense of belonging and cohesion that is greater than any of the individual members. However, this process is even more extreme for the young person because developmentally these children do not know themselves outside of these groups. That is, the group is an important part of the identity of youth, both those in collective-oriented and individual-oriented societies. As such, to move outside the group means certain pain, because to remove this scaffold would mean to remove sense of self, and, in many unsafe areas in the United States and in war-affected areas around the world, to move outside the group may mean lack of safety from attack and even death. Following on this point, the group is often central to shaping and even dictating the behavior of the individual, as Merari has pointed out. The power of the group is so magnanimous that the young person has finds it very appealing to submit. What began as an altruistic wish to serve the group becomes an imperative.

CHAPTER 4

When Will the War End? "Never."

When the Last Tamil Has Died

We interviewed young people in Sri Lanka whom we met through a network procedure. We promised anonymity. We make no claim that this is a random or even representative group. We can say that they were in school, living in relative safety, and that many of them had had past experiences of loss and displacement. In that respect they were probably not unlike many young students on the island.

The young people (ages of 13 to 18) we interviewed looked and acted a lot like American teenagers might have acted—a lot like my children and their friends acted at the same age. They giggled. They wanted to be interviewed with their friends, not alone. They were curious and funny, telling jokes, smiling, and gently teasing one another. They were regular, appealing, teenagers, by turns shy and outspoken, concerned about clothes and appearance, music, Hollywood, and friendship. They were thoughtful, and they even risked an occasional comment that was a little bit bold or challenging. We could have fooled ourselves into thinking we were interviewing children somewhere more familiar to us. We could have fooled ourselves into thinking the children before us had never known war, danger, or loss. That is, until we started asking serious questions, and they started providing serious answers.

When Will the War End? "Never"

Hope for a speedy end to the long ethnic war is hard to come by in Sri Lanka. It was not surprising to us that half of the elders we talked to did not think they would live to see peace. Perhaps we should not have been surprised when we heard distressingly similar comments from these adolescents who, moments

earlier, had been singing and joking—who now told us they did not expect peace to come in their lifetimes. Living in a war zone surely reduces the average life expectancy, and early death is part of everyday life in such war-affected areas. We do not know whether their answers reflected a shortened life expectancy, anticipation of a very long war, or perhaps both. Other researchers have reported that children living in war zones do not expect to have a long life. Distressing as it was to hear children say they would not see peace, the most stunning, distressing, answer to that question came when a teenager matter-of-factly predicted that the war would not end until the day "When the last Tamil has died."

We think it unlikely that there will some day be no Tamils in Sri Lanka, but if the teenagers thought the government planned to kill all members of the Tamil Tigers, they were not, apparently, far off. The Sri Lankan Daily News recently reported that Sri Lankan military commanders predicted the "extinction" of the Tamil Tigers in 2008.[1] The government of Sri Lanka formally ended the cease-fire with the LTTE which had been negotiated in 2002, with the help of Norway, and monitoring mission representatives have left the island.

While killing all the LTTE rebels is not the same as killing all Tamils, the children's lack of hope surely reflected the reality that things were not going well in Sri Lanka, and may have reflected both awareness of the government's intention as well as a belief that it would be thwarted. The government has evidently decided that, at this time, not negotiation, but killing all the Tamil fighters, is the best method available. The LTTE, meanwhile, claims, officially, to be willing to comply with the 2002 cease-fire terms. They portray themselves as committed to self-determination, which, they think, is the most likely way to achieve freedom and equality for Tamils. At least this is how they portray themselves to the outside world. It is not clear whether this is credible to those in or out of the country.

What Will It Be Like When the War Ends?

While, on the whole, the children we interviewed did not expect peace any time soon, they did have vivid images of what they hoped and predicted peace would be like. Personal hopes and individual beliefs about life after war are possible for older children, who have the ability to imagine things different from the way they are—not simply stating a conventional line, not repeating a slogan or cliche, but creating their own images. They told us that the end of war would mean the end of conflict among the groups (Sinhalese, Tamil, and Muslim) and people would be together again. The children we interviewed expressed no animosity toward members of any ethnic groups, and clearly they saw the possibility of such reunion—or perhaps union, since they had known only a brief moment when the groups got along, a moment just after the tsunami, when the situation was so dire that differences had been ignored. They attributed responsibility for the war to the government of Sri Lanka—not the Sinhalese

people—and to the soldiers representing that government. Some of the children we interviewed also attributed responsibility to other governments or people who helped or supported the government, such as by providing money or arms, or selling arms to the government. They did not blame Sinhalese, Tamil, or Muslim civilians. This is an important point, in that it hints at the possibility that, once the war ends, peace among ethnic groups in Sri Lanka is likely to be a real possibility—not something peacekeepers will have to monitor endlessly.

The children also told us that once the war ended, everyone could go back to their homes. Like many other Americans, we had not allowed ourselves to think seriously about the dreaded experience of displacement as one of the major costs of war. We may not have thought much about it, but the children clearly had, and some had experienced it. Fortunately, the translator for this study made sure every child was asked about it. Having to leave one's home and community is a frequent occurrence in the war-affected areas of Sri Lanka, and in all other countries affected by war. Massive displacements are apt to have an especially devastating effect in a collectivist culture such as Sri Lanka. Displacements—sometimes the same family must manage several displacements—reflect a cost of war that is hardly ever talked about by those of us lucky enough not to live in a war-affected area (Wessells 2006, p. 47; Rosen 2005, p. 7).

Of course, it is a lovely fantasy to think that at the end of war, everyone would go back to the same homes they had lived in before the war, and live in the same neighborhoods, with the same neighbors who were there before. Lovely image, but impossible in reality. Homes would be destroyed. People would have died. Family members would have become too poor, sick, maimed, or injured to return home. Some of the ways people made a living would no longer be available. Children would be orphaned. In some cases, the neighborhoods would be unrecognizable. Roads to the areas would have been blown up and, in those very poor countries where ethnic wars go on and on, there is not likely to be money available to quickly rebuild them. Some entire communities would have so many land mines that they would be uninhabitable. In others, the families would not be allowed to return simply because the forces opposing their group would not allow them to return. In some instances, governments have ideas about rebuilding after destruction that do not include allowing people to rebuild where they were before, since some other use for the land too might be considered to be more beneficial.

That these barely imaginable things are happening to real people—adults not unlike our families and neighbors, and children who are so remarkably like our own children, even though they are halfway around the world from them causes Americans to want to think about something else. It is too uncomfortable to contemplate. We want to believe that someone is doing something about this. The Red Cross, maybe, or UNICEF. Many such organizations are trying to help. The need, around the world, is great—more than great, unimaginably huge—and surely cannot ever be met by all possible humanitarian efforts, even on a

global scale. Indeed, they could not be met even if things were simple and straightforward, and trucks could go deliver provisions consistently safely, and so on. Whereas, in fact, things are anything but simple and straightforward.

Should Americans talk about these things? Would it be useful? My colleague Steven Zeitlin believes that the issues around talking about terrorism in American families in this decade closely parallel those that arose in the 1980s when the nuclear threat was immediate and on the minds of many adults, and yet had become a topic that was taboo in family conversations (Steven Zeitlin, pers. comm., March 2008). Indeed, nuclear weapons are again a threat, and that threat is now interwoven with terrorist threats, since it now seems possible that a nuclear weapon might be obtained by a group that is willing and able to engage in terrorist actions. Some would argue that nuclear warfare is, by definition, terrorism, since the use of such a weapon would undoubtedly kill mostly civilians, create panic, and draw massive attention. (This, then, leads back to the controversial question about whether actions sponsored by governments can be called terrorism.)

Zeitlin, together with David Greenwald, videotaped twenty-five families as they attempted to talk about the nuclear threat. They learned that many of the children had thought a great deal about the nuclear threat—much more than their parents realized, and that the worry that kept parents from mentioning it to children—the worry of disturbing or upsetting the children by mentioning it, was ill-founded, since they were already worried, and at the same time felt they had no one to talk to about it. Of great importance here, they found that, at least in their sample, children were relieved when the topic was talked about, and felt much better when they knew their parents were thinking and even working on solving the problems.

Greenwald and Zeitlin concluded that one of the terrible costs of the nuclear threat was that parents were made to feel helpless and unable to protect their children; thus this technological development that was capable of destroying the world was already destroying the natural order of the older generation caring for the younger generation, keeping them safe. This disruption in the parental role was exacerbated when parents, with good intention, decided not to talk about nuclear weapons with their children. It is our observation that a similar difficulty is occurring right now, in that parents do not know how to talk to their children about this terrible threat and fear of terrorism—something they cannot control and from which, they fear, they cannot protect their children.

The Irony of a Common Theme

So the very difficulties faced by parents in war-affected areas—that they cannot properly or adequately protect their children—is parallel to the difficulties faced by those in less directly affected areas. Parents in war-affected areas cannot be certain that they can educate their children, or protect their children, and cannot

even be sure they will be able to feed or provide shelter for them. Parents in indirectly affected areas cannot guarantee the safety of their children against terrorist acts. And parents in either directly or indirectly affected areas cannot protect their children against nuclear war, or against the horrors of contemplating it. Indeed, the same terrible events that interfere with parents protecting their children in the war-affected areas eventually interfere with all parents' ability to protect their children. Is it too simple to say that this is evidence of the small world we inhabit, and that we who would let children and families be torn apart by war anywhere may pay a very steep price at home?

Talking About It

On the other hand, Greenwald and Zeitlin found that the children in the families they met felt better if they knew that their parents were concerned and were actively working to stop the nuclear threat. Perhaps the same is true for children all around the world whose parents work against violence, war, and terrorism.

Freedom to Travel

The children we interviewed told us not only that they wanted everyone to return to their homes, but that, once there, they should be free to travel away from and back to those homes. They said that when there was peace they would feel freer, and that people would be able to travel, on the island or off. Some children got a bit carried away, telling us that once the war was over, they would be able to travel anywhere, anytime, even at midnight, without fear—an image that we loved, though we doubted the likelihood of it coming about any time soon in Sri Lanka or in the United States.

At the time we interviewed the children, people were not free to travel. There were numerous checkpoints on the road, and trains and buses were frequently stopped, the passengers required to wait in long lines, even in extremely hot weather, to show identification. Checkpoints that led out of minority areas and into majority areas tended here, as they do in other parts of the world where there is ethnic war, to take quite a long time to travel through. Tamils believe that Sinhalese are allowed to pass through checkpoints easily, while they are not, and not only in the war-affected northeast. As for travel out of the country, it was unthinkable for the children we met, and for the Tamil adults we met, as well. With very few exceptions, even if by something close to a miracle they could get enough money together, they almost certainly could not get visas. It was, frankly, heartbreaking to realize that virtually none of the people we met could actually come to visit us here in the United States. A few could travel on holiday, if sponsored, but it would take a great deal of effort and planning to obtain the necessary permissions.

The Privilege of an Education

Consistent with adults in areas of unrest, the children identified opportunities for education as a benefit of peace, and the disruption of education that many children experienced as a cost of war. They looked forward to a time when education was more accessible to all young people—once the war was over. They said this despite the fact that the children we interviewed were all in school. (We set this condition, as well as a condition that the children be safe, for ourselves so as not to put any children who were not safe at increased risk, and also not to open up painful topics with children who needed to cope with ongoing immediate fear and danger. It is widely believed that when children are at imminent risk, they need all their available mental resources to cope with the risk, and that may include the freedom to deny that there is any risk or avoid talking about it, so as to maintain some emotional equilibrium. Despite their being safe and in school, however, virtually none of the children we met would be able to attend university, no matter how hard they studied, how good their grades were, or how much potential they showed, because of lack of funds, ongoing war and disruption and, in some cases, they would not be able to pursue the education they wished, it was their understanding, simply because they were Tamil.

While we required that the children we talked to were safe, we also realized that safety is not only relative, but, sadly, is not a permanent condition, when you live in a war zone. Today we worry a great deal about the children who were safe several months ago. We do not know if they are still safe. They are almost certainly at greater risk now than they were before the government announced it was unilaterally ending the cease-fire. This is how ethnic wars go—variable in their intensity. Today you are safe, for now. Tomorrow? You might be in the wrong place. Your school might be too close to where the bus blows up. You might enter an area where, unbeknownst to you, someone has just set off a bomb, and you might be misidentified as someone who might have been involved. You might be shot on sight. Are wars never settled, then? In recent memory, the war in Northern Ireland seems to have been settled, with great courage and the acceptance of great risk on the part of the leaders of various factions and careful planning including ongoing monitoring. Their risks paid off, with things continuing to get better, even years past the cease-fire. However, there are contrasting examples in many parts of the world.

We thought the lack of hope for peace reflected in these responses, together with the things the children we interviewed had witnessed, and the vivid images of how things could be better, and the many stories of frustrated attempts to achieve fundamental goals, might help explain why children—if not the ones we interviewed, then children whose experiences were just a little worse—might be willing to join a fighting force of some kind, thinking, as they might, that it would bring the war to a victorious close sooner. Perhaps the importance of the

cause, as perceived by a child, would justify joining up. Perhaps the frustrations and uncertainties of life as usual would be easy to give up in favor of a chance to be proactive. Perhaps they felt that their fates were sealed, but those of their younger brothers, sisters, or cousins were not.

How Old Should Someone Be Before Joining a Fighting Force?

Various international groups, notably the United Nations, set eighteen as the minimum age for entry into a militia or army. We asked some children and adults in Sri Lanka how old they thought someone should be before joining a fighting force. We were deliberately vague about which fighting force we might have in mind. The average age provided by a child in response to that question was eighteen and a half years. That was the average, but the range was quite wide, with some children suggesting a good age would be fourteen, and others twenty-five. When we asked adults the same question, the average response was just under nineteen years, with the range being from fifteen to twenty-seven and a half. When we asked our small sample of adults whether they would change their answer if the group was fighting for a very good cause, none changed their answer. The children, however, did, and the average age at which they thought it would be ok for someone to join a fighting force for a very good cause was just over sixteen years, with a range of answers from ten to twenty years. Our sample was not random, large, or representative, so we cannot say for sure whether it applies to most children in most war zones, or even most children in Sri Lanka, but it is consistent with the development of children's thinking and reasoning processes and with the manner in which, neuropsychologists are now learning, adolescents approach risk. (This was discussed in chapter 3.)

While most of the world's humanitarian agencies agree on the age of 18 as the minimum age when someone should be allowed to enter a fighting force, or recruited to join a fighting force, it is clear that this criterion does not fit with all communities' or societies' views. Wessells believes that this age standard should be maintained even in the face of disagreement or lack of fit with community standards. Rosen, by contrast, questions the universal application of this standard. Most compelling among his arguments: that children in a genocide situation had better be allowed to fight, and had better choose to fight, as that may greatly increase their chances of survival. Rosen and the United Nations are both right, of course. There should be a standard, and the standard should be overlooked when a child has such a terrible choice: fight or face certain death.

On the one hand, the universal application of this age criterion might seem naïve, but Wessells is anything but naïve. Indeed, he may well be the most experienced and knowledgeable expert on child soldiers in the West today. In our view, a standard is critical, and all countries and militias should keep to it. At the same time, people of good will should break it when (and, crucially, only

when) the alternative is certain—or near certain—death for the child. We were told before our research in Sri Lanka that, at least in the past, the LTTE forcibly recruited boys when they turned fifteen. On the other hand, some government forces (evidently nonsystematically) killed boys just before they turned fifteen, in order to deny the LTTE the opportunity to have one more soldier. It is clear what the international bodies must do: bring pressure to bear on both the LTTE and the government, and that is just what they did and continue to do. However, if you were not an international agency representative, but just a parent facing such a hideous situation, what would you do? If you were a parent, displaced into a refugee camp, and your daughter was at grave risk of being raped and abused, there was inadequate security, and she came to you and said she wanted to join a militia, what judgment could you make? Suppose it was a militia where girls fought side by side with boys, were fed well, and not at risk of rape. What would you say? Boarding school is not an option. Leaving the situation is not an option. She cannot get a visa. There is no safe way to leave. Will you tell her to wait till she turns eighteen? There are no easy answers—no formula will do. Surely you would not care what the United Nations or any other agency had to say about it.

Growing Up in War-Affected Areas

With all our clinical, academic, and experiential expertise combined, we began to have the very beginnings of a sense of what it would be like to grow up in a war zone. We know of no research studies where the researchers have followed children living in war-affected areas over long periods of time. Although Briggs did return to reinterview some of the children he met when researching child soldiers, the time between interviews was long, the interviews were not systematic, and the first interview had taken place after the child was already a soldier. We thought it would be important to put together all we know about the children of the world who become engaged in terrorist actions—not only in Sri Lanka be in all the places with child soldiers that we know about—especially those who become engaged in actions involving planful death of the attacker. Our goal is to begin to construct a model of the life of a child in a war-affected area, beginning from a young age. We wanted to begin to build this model because we came to believe that we could understand the circumstances that might contribute to a child becoming a soldier, and we wanted others to understand, as well. We came to believe that many Americans had conceptualized children who engaged in terrorist acts as either mentally ill, impaired, or without adequate protection, guidance, and love from their families. By contrast, we had begun to think of children who engaged in terrorist acts as either unwilling victims who were forcefully recruited, or as partially willing victims, intentionally engaging in a desperate attempt to end a bad situation, if not for themselves, then for those who came after. We thought of their actions as wrong and terribly harmful.

We thought of their parents as woefully unable to exercise their potential for parental caretaking, and we could, especially after 9/11, when we were dramatically reminded of the limits of our own abilities to protect our own children, relate to that in some way.

We pored over our data in the context of all we had observed during the visit to Sri Lanka, all we had learned about terrorism practiced there and in other parts of the world, and all we knew about child and adolescent development. We established a working model of what it is like to be a child growing up as a member of the minority—or weaker—party in an ongoing local war. How would an atmosphere of war look and feel to someone growing up in the midst of it? We checked our model against first person accounts, scholarship, and fictionalized accounts of children affected by war, and reports from humanitarian agencies. We believe this is about as close as any Western social science scholar has come or can come, given the present state of social science knowledge, to describing the common factors present in many war zones for children growing up—we are working here to establish that missing prototype of the history of a young terrorist. We hope our first attempt at a model will be the beginning of a series of better and better models for the development of child soldiers who engage in terrorist actions in which the plan is for them to die. We also think that it will be clearer why a child might volunteer, as well as why a child who does not volunteer might become engaged in suicide/martyr acts, once one can understand what the life of a child in a war zone is like. Here is the long and short of it: We think that the step a child must take from growing up in the midst of violence to performing an act of violence is, very sadly, a short one. Here is our model.

Ethnic Conflict: An Informed Account of a (Fictional) Minority Child's Experience

If you are a child who has never known peace, you do not wonder whether tomorrow will bring an end to war; you are not holding your breath. It is not exactly that you are cynical, or even depressed about it. War is a fact of life: the sounds, the smells, the sights. Like children in poor and unsafe neighborhoods in the United States, children in areas affected by war do not, at first, realize that their lives are harder than average, and that there is no fairness to who has a hard life and who has an easy one. Young children of but a few years are not likely to make such comparisons, especially if most of their family, neighbors, and friends are in circumstances similar to their own. Jonathon Kozol (1992, p. 52), observer of poor American children and families for several decades, has noted that it is not until about age 10 that children begin to realize that there is structural inequality—inequality that is built into the system. Although it is clear from Kozol's work, however, that the realization of structural inequality has a very big impact on children, principles of developmental psychology help us

understand that younger children, who do not yet have the capacity to imagine an alternate world, would be less likely to notice that things are not as they should be.

At the very youngest ages, then, children growing up in war-affected areas are not aware that some children grow up without the sounds, sights, smells, and feel of war. Beyond that, however, young children's experiences in war-affected areas are structured by the fact that they are not feared. Since young children are generally not feared by soldiers—not by either those in power or those challenging the status quo—and they are generally not expected to attack anyone, their experience is different from older children in war zones, where the older children might be seen as potential attackers. (There are some exceptions—places where despicable adults use very young children as attackers who are bound to die in the attack, or as bait to lure the enemy to a place that will be blown up, knowing the children, along with the enemy, will die. Children of the opposition ethnic, religious, or political group in those places may be feared, but those places are somewhat exceptional.) Mostly, young children have a different experience from older children in war-affected areas, both because the young children are not feared and also because they are simply not old enough to understand yet that the larger world might be very different from their own. It takes a while before children learn that things they experience are different from what others experience, and even longer to realize that it is unfair.

We attempt here to portray life from the point of view of a child living in a war-affected area. Since this has not been attempted before, we realize that we will not get everything exactly right. But we do believe we have a good basis for beginning a project to understand what it feels like to grow up in a war-affected area, and we hope others will contribute to this effort, correcting our errors and adding where we have incomplete information.

From the Child's Point of View: Very Young Children in War-Affected Areas

You live in a certain village. You have been loved and cared for as an infant—not only by your parents, but by other family members, friends, and neighbors. Now that you can walk and talk and even leave your family's house to walk to a nearby house, you do certain things during the day—perhaps you help family members, or elders. Your father works to provide things for your family, maybe as a fisherman or shop owner. Maybe your family owns some land, or maybe they work for someone who does. You go some places with family members. You play with other children, both younger and older than yourself. The older children teach you things. Sometimes they teach you about right from wrong; other times they teach you secrets, but you must promise to keep that from adults. You do the same for the younger children, when you have a chance. That happens when

the older children are busy, or do not see the need for intervention. You do what the older children have done for you. When you go about your village, you see certain things: Markets, roadside stands, animals, buses, food, drinks, old men and women, and younger men and women, and children. People at work. People eating. Sometimes resting. You see places people gather to pray. There are cows and motorcycles on the road. You find things to play with. Maybe, if you are very, very fortunate, you can look forward to some day going to school. You hope so. Your parents hope so—in fact they pray for that. You see some children go to school, some days.

You may or may not be allowed to ask questions of the elders. You must be respectful. You do not expect grown-up people to be happy, and on the rare occasions when they are, it is exciting, but it does not last long. Sometimes you hear adults talking and they sound worried, but they do not let you know what is causing the worry. If your family is fortunate, you usually have enough to eat, but you know that sometimes some other people are hungry and do not have enough. Sometimes your family invites others to share their food. You must never mention it if there is really not quite enough to go around and you are still hungry. That would be frowned on.

And there are soldiers. When you are young and playful, the soldiers do not much bother with you, and may even smile at you. But they are not as easy on your older brothers and sisters, your parents, or the other adults. You hear adults whispering about it, and they instruct you on how to conduct yourself around the soldiers. They may even warn or threaten you, implying that bad things will happen if you disobey the soldiers. But you do not yet fear the soldiers. In the world you know, there are some dangers. You could drown if you go too far out in the water; you could get bitten if you play with dogs in the street; and you may be told you could be kidnapped by the soldiers, especially if you disobey them. It is easy to imagine that dogs might turn out to be mean, or that water could turn out to be deeper than you thought, but it is hard to imagine, at first, soldiers treating you badly. Perhaps you have heard of soldiers kidnapping other children, older than you. You imagine those children did something wrong. Sometimes the soldiers shout and get angry. You could maybe get hurt if you get between the soldiers and someone they are shouting at, if you get too close when there is trouble, but it is not hard to stay away. You know your mother will be tense around the soldiers, and you accept it as a fact of life, though you do not yet understand. Your strong father will act very quiet around the soldiers. Later he will be angry, or he might drink a lot. The soldiers carry guns, but you do not see them shoot. You often hear guns firing, though, those must be of some other soldiers or someone who is not a soldier. Occasionally you notice the old people looking sad, telling stories, even crying a little, but when they see you they brighten up. They are glad to see you, and they do not let you see them sad for more than a moment, if they can help it, if they see you watching.

There are things you can and cannot do. Perhaps you cannot cross a particular street, or go out after dark, or play in certain places, or disobey a soldier. Some family or friends you know have had to leave their homes, because of what the adults call "the situation" and live with other family members or in camps. There is a lot to cope with, a lot to navigate. But you just do not spend a lot of time wondering whether there will soon be less to cope with. Soldiers, guns, ammunition—it is all out there, a fact of life; war is one reality you can count on. On the days when there are no sounds of war, you are aware of something missing.

In the meantime, you are learning certain values from your elders: Be kind; take care of others; cooperate; value school; obey and respect elders; tell the truth; be generous; work hard; be fair; love God; the importance of helping your family and community everyday. There are tales—call them folk tales—that warn you of the bad results that have occurred when someone was too greedy or too proud. You hear those many times, and you want to hear them again. You are taught to make your family proud. Yet you can begin to see that there is some sort of puzzle here, because the values you are taught do not seem to be the same that some other people are using, especially the soldiers and police. They are living by some other set; you cannot name them, but you see them: threat, power, violence, greed, crudeness, bad language, unfairness—the exact opposite of what you learn is right. Still, they treat you well. Occasionally they even call you over to give you something. Your parents let you take things the soldiers offer, but they do not laugh with the soldiers. But you are small and you know there are some things you do not understand. You wait for it all to be clear. You do not worry about it because it is a grown-up kind of thing, and you feel that someone must understand it all now, and you will soon.

There are many mysteries when you are growing up in a war-affected area. Sometimes people disappear or do not come around. You might start to ask about them, and get the idea that you are being impolite. You stop. Perhaps one of the older children will tell you what you want to know, but probably not. "When will my uncle come?" You may want to ask, but the stern looks on the faces of the adults around you tell you it was not a good question to ask, and your grandmother is starting to cry. Where is the man who used to bring fish? And you are hushed. Such has been your life as a lucky young child in a war-affected area, for the early years.

But if you are a young child in a war zone, at some point war gets too close and the adults cannot protect you from knowing about the bad things. Your brother signs up for a militia. He tells you he is leaving to help the people, but to you it means he is going away, and everyone, including you, is a little sad. Besides, you do not understand why he has to go away to help, since the people right nearby need help.

Maybe your father will be killed by soldiers who are suspicious, angry, or drunk with power—perhaps they make you watch. Perhaps they shot him. Perhaps it was much worse—more gruesome. You try not to cry, because the

elders tell you he is with God, or that you have to be strong for your sisters. You try not to remember it, but it keeps coming back, especially when you hear guns somewhere. You wonder if your father did something bad. Or if you did something bad that made this terrible thing happen. Perhaps you were too greedy. The soldiers and guards you see on the street do not look so harmless now, even if they smile at you. The ones who used to see you smile now think you have changed and call you the somber one. You never smile at them. You want to spit at them, but you know that you cannot do that. You do not understand why they are surprised that you do not smile—don't they know?

You hear about a girl you knew, older than you, whom a soldier hurt in some way and now she says she is his wife. She is going to have a baby—a soldier's baby. You wonder what a soldier's baby might look like, but you think you had better not ask. Another girl is threatened by a young member of a fighting group. Your mother is distraught by something she saw or heard about, and becomes depressed and moody. You try to cheer her up. Some teenagers come to your home and threaten to take your sister away if your family does not give them a certain amount of food or money. Or soldiers come and wake you up at night to ask a lot of questions and then tell your family they are taking over your house and you all have to get up and leave the house, in the night. They may hurt your mother or father even though it is clear they are obeying the soldiers—you are all getting out. They may say your parents are not moving fast enough. They may look at you as if you are not moving fast enough. Your brother tries to protect you. They hit him. They scare everyone. Your mother may be bleeding but she says she is ok. You do not see your cousin—did the soldiers take him? It is dark, and perhaps you are lucky enough to find another home to sleep in, or perhaps your family has to walk a long distance to a camp. Someone you know tries to leave the area, tries to get far away by boat, but the boat is shot at, and the people drown. These things your family tries to keep from you. They want you to stay cheerful, but some things they cannot keep from you. Once your family moves to a camp, you cannot go to school and some days there is not enough food. There are people with white skin who speak some other language and they are in charge of food. They are weary. They smile at you, and some of them look very tired and worried. On better days, you can ask questions of the one with yellow hair. She knows a little of your language. You know a little of hers, too, but you do not tell her that yet.

Your cousin burns to death in a fire caused by a bomb. You have heard about these things before, but when they get too close, it is very hard to continue coping. At the same time, as a child, you have no power to do anything but keep coping as best you can. You no longer look forward to going to school—it is all you can do to help your mother and keep her from crying.

Some psychologists react to this part of the story by wanting to help those children cope. Or at least help their caretakers know how to help them.

We know a lot about treating acute stress and longer-term post-traumatic stress. They ask: Can we send enough mental health workers to help the children? But they must remind themselves that we do not know how to help children cope when the fundamental conditions of safety are not met, and when, any hour or minute, a new trauma may occur. We do not know how to make people feel safe when they are not safe, nor would we want to.

Should we try to remove the children, as was done during the bombing in Europe during World War II? Even if the parents agreed, how would it affect the community if we removed the children at risk?

It is our best judgment that everyone, mental health workers included, can make the biggest impact on the situations like those in Sri Lanka, by instructing their governments and international bodies to monitor and intervene, and to encourage negotiated solutions to ongoing intra-country conflict.

We discuss this further in the final chapter of this book.

Middle Childhood

By the time you are ten or so years old, you are very likely to be aware that you and your family have been badly affected by the war, or if you have been very very lucky and have not personally been affected, someone you know well, possibly someone in your family, has been. You have begun to learn some things in school or from your friends about the war. You are becoming aware that there are other children in other countries who do not have the same sorts of problems that you and your family have. They do not have wars or soldiers. You cannot really imagine what life would be like if you were as lucky as they are, but you are beginning to get a picture. Someone has a sister who went to a city and had access to the Internet or a TV or cell phone, and somehow you heard about life in such places. Every child has a phone. Everyone even has their own television and computer. They have fancy cars. You have seen photos of those cars. You are beginning to try to make sense of it. You imagine the people must be very happy. They can travel, too. You are also becoming aware of the fact that your people—your family, village, community, church, school—are in some way being treated in an unfair way, just because of who they are. Because of things they cannot change. Things they did not choose. You are beginning to realize that in some way there is luck in the world and you and those you know have had too much bad luck. Perhaps you think that if only you and the other children are nicer, behave better, work harder, that this will shift and better luck will come along. You might try.

Sometimes you wonder whether those other children, who have so much, know about you, or care. There are younger children who do not know anything

much about the world yet. There are older children who know more. Many are angry. Some are sad. The adults have told them things that you do not yet know. There are times you wish you did not know. You see your little brothers and cousins and they are happier than you. You may be lucky and some day have a chance to go to school again, but for now you cannot go because your mother needs you at home. When you went to school, the teachers were pretty and clean and cheerful. Your favorite, a young one, is no longer in your village. There is no school now. It is now a place where food is kept and given to families who are hungry. Sometimes you get food from there. The food sometimes gets very low, and then you wait for a truck to come, bringing more. Every so often it is very late, and people get hungry. What would it be like to have a market again?

At night, some nights, the adults still sing and play music. Life is good then. No one is worrying. No one is sick. That happens on the days when the navy lets people fish again, for one day, things are happy.

Older Children: Thirteen and Beyond

At around thirteen, you begin to think differently. You imagine what-ifs, you begin to understand how things in the world interact. At some point, things change if you are a child living in war, because you begin to get bigger and begin to mature. The ever present soldiers start to look at you differently. You look like a threat to them now. It happens gradually. They start to ask you more questions. They do not smile so much. They stop you and make you show ID, even if they knew who you were last year, even if they have known you for several years. They do not follow the rules of politeness you have learned. You try to protect the littler children from the soldiers. In school, if you go to school, you learn that the soldiers represent the government and are keeping the town safe, but it does not feel safe.

You have learned about history, not only the history of your own village and your own country, but of the interactions between the West and the East, between the rich countries in Europe and North America and the poor countries, like yours. You learn about wars, about alliances. Exactly what you learn depends on whom you learned it from. It might be from older kids, from teachers, from your parents or their friends, or from the religious leaders. Even from some of the aid workers. Some things might not sound quite right. There have been good leaders and bad ones. There were times when other countries owned your country and ordered everyone around. There was a king, far away, who possibly never even came to your country, who decided everything. The people in your country felt lucky if people from the king's country liked them. They tried to please the people from the king's country. The people from the king's country taught them things, and if they were servants in the homes of the people, they were lucky. Or if they had a good job, it was working for someone from the king's country.

They owned everything. You cannot understand how the people of your country put up with someone from another country ordering them around, owning their land. It does not make a lot of sense, to you, but you are not supposed to ask too many questions yet.

You learn too that the king's country—whichever one applies to your country—just decided one day that he could not run your country anymore. Some of the people from that country went home. Then the people in your country started fighting over who would be in charge. They are still fighting. Things are not fair. Your people are smart and can do things, but the other people are in charge, and they keep things for themselves. You find this out from listening to the grown-ups and older kids talk. Your people are not free. They cannot do what they want to do. They cannot go to school. They cannot own the land. They are poor. Things are very bad, and they are worse for your people than for the others. Worst of all, your people were here first, but they still cannot be free. Now the government tries to keep your people from getting power. They do it with an army.

You may very well know that the boats, planes, rifles, uniforms you see around you were purchased using money from other countries of the world. You may also know which countries. And you begin to see those other countries as troublesome, as meddlers, and worse.

Truth and Lies

When you are thirteen, there are not a lot of shades of grey. Things are truth or lies, right or wrong, good or bad. You do not yet know that two things that appear to contradict each other can both be true, or both be false. You do not know that the truth can be subtle, that sometimes it is not absolute. You do not know that there can be enemies and both sides of a conflict may have a good point, at least from their own point of view, and that neither side may be all good or all bad.

You have heard about a different kind of soldier, soldiers you do not see because they usually hide. Your family may forbid you to talk about them, but your friends and you talk about them. You know they fight against the soldiers you see everyday. You might think it is a good idea for someone to be against the soldiers you see. From your point of view, those soldiers you see everyday scare the adults around you, and make life complicated for everyone. They do not follow rules, except the ones the older soldiers give them, and they make everyone do whatever they say. Some of them have been quite mean, and you have heard that they have done really terrible things. You have heard that they do not like you or anyone in your neighborhood or community because you are members of a certain group, but there is no good reason for them to dislike your group. You know from your own experience with them that they can treat people badly, even kids like you.

By the time you are about thirteen years old, even if you have been incredibly lucky, and no one you know has been terribly affected by the war, you know a great deal about the soldiers and what they represent. The things you have seen and been told before start to form a picture. It is not a happy picture. It is also not a complete picture, but you do not know that yet. When you are thirteen years old, right and wrong seem very very clear. The soldiers represent people who annoy, scare, and order your family around. They are from the powerful side, the free side, the side that is not treating you or your family well. They are from the side that gets the money and gets to go to school. They look tough and if you allow yourself to think of what it would be like to be a soldier, you find it exciting. You would feel strong, powerful, invincible. The opposite of how most of the people you know feel, including you. And at the same time it is hateful. They cause old people to stand in the hot sun and wait while they look at everyone's ID. They do not respect even elders, and yet they get away with it.

But you know you can never be one of those visible soldiers. Not because you are not big enough, strong enough, smart enough, determined enough. Because you were born part of the opposite side—part of the weaker side. It is not fair, and when you are thirteen, fairness is very important. You know fairness is right, and you have been taught it over and over, but it does not seem that the adults really get how unfairly they are being treated, or how unfairly they are treating other people.

Those soldiers look at you as if they own you. It makes you angry, and it makes the girls scared. But you must not react. You must ignore their looks. You watch the older girls and boys; that is what they do. Or is it possible they do not even notice the hatred for the boys or the desire for the girls? At times you think you cannot take it another minute.

If you eavesdrop on adults, you learn that you and your family and the other families were better off in some past—a very long time ago. In those days, they were respected. They had things to do, took care of their families, ran their own communities, looked after the poor and the sick and elderly. They had their own medicines and enough resources. Maybe the men hunted, or fished, and took things to markets, the women grew vegetables and fruit, and cooked. Life was better in the past, long before the soldiers came. There were no checkpoints. You learn that they think the soldiers enjoy making them miserable. And you are angry, but do not know what to do.

The thing that is becoming very clear to you is that there has been a lot of unfairness, and it has affected people like you, people you know and love. You wonder whether those other soldiers—the ones who fight against the soldiers you have seen everyday since you were a toddler—the ones your cousin, or friend, joined, can make things right for your people. You go about your life, doing what you do and what is expected of you, and you listen hard to try to understand.

A little more time goes by and your body is growing. You have some new feelings, and new responsibilities too. You can no longer do everything that other people of your age do, now your role as a young man or young woman gives you possibilities and limits too. Your parents and aunts keep telling you how good looking you are, and how capable you will be. People look at you differently, now, and expect more of you and you are happy to be able to provide it. You are stronger and can reach further. You can begin to take care of your family in certain ways. You can help your family more, and that makes everything easier for them, and makes them happy.

Sometimes things are calm and you almost forget about the war and about the unfairness, and the countries who are at fault. But other times you hear about awful things happening, and you get angry, and sad, and confused. You know about this other army, and maybe you have heard of some things they have done, but none as bad, and certainly none worse, than the things the soldiers you know do.

Of course, during this time you are beginning to think of yourself as a potential parent, a potential adult, a potential lover. You are wondering what sort of job you might have—if you might be able to have one. You are wondering if you will live long enough to have such a job.

Things You Know; Things You Do not Know

As a young teenager, you believe that you know quite a lot. You also believe that the adults in your family do not have any idea how much you do know; in fact, they do not even know many of the things you know. You see that they have been basically good people, and look where it has gotten them. Even your father, who is brave and strong, and who makes decisions in your family, obeys every little thing the soldiers say. And the soldiers—they are not nice people. They have done nothing to earn respect. Quite the opposite. They deserve to be hated.

You think your generation can do better than your parents, but you are not sure your friends have the courage. They like to play it safe; they are afraid of the soldiers too. All that respect, all that fear, earned by a gun—nothing else. You know there are people who are trying to change things. Trying to end the war. But ending the war will be nothing if it leaves you and your family and friends at the mercy of soldiers and the government just like it is now. You will have no pride and no future. You will not be able to protect your children or even feed them.

If only you were president, or if your uncle or aunt were president, things would be better. You would make it right. You would talk to the soldiers. You would tell everyone that from that day on, everyone is free and everyone is equal. You think that whoever is in power must be very stupid or very evil to keep things the way they are. But then of course, you will never be in power. You will never

be president. You cannot even go to school or college. You cannot even prevent your cousins or sisters from being hurt or kidnapped. It happens. And then one day something happens—another thing. Maybe the worst thing, or maybe something that is no worse than a hundred other things, but it is the thing that changes everything.

It All Looks Clear Now

Maybe today you heard that the government blew up a school, and children were killed. Or that the soldiers kidnapped someone. Maybe someone you know was raped by the soldiers, or shot. Maybe your cousin drowned after the navy shot at his fishing boat. You do not think these things would ever happen to people of the other group—the group in power. Maybe you were stopped and talked to in a particularly demeaning way. Maybe they searched all your pockets and made fun of you.

Somewhere, somehow, you have heard of this other fighting force. The LTTE or FARC or ETA or whatever your local militia might be. Everything you hear about them in the newspapers or radio is bad. They are killers, blowing up airports and nightclubs, killing people. But you cannot believe those newspapers or radios. The government lies, and everyone knows it.

In private, you hear a different story: They are fighting to free the people you love from the tyrannical government, from the unfair laws, from the lack of opportunity, and from the ever-present, ever-annoying soldiers. You learn from these private sources that they are the good side, they dedicate their lives to helping people. They are the brave, selfless, strong ones. And they do not intimidate the public. They need more people to help with this cause. They need strong, young people. If you are a girl, you also learn that even girls in this militia can be real soldiers, carry guns, and go into battle. There is a camp where you learn. Someone can help you find it. This militia has guns, bombs, boats, and trucks. They will let you come and learn. Then you decide. That is what you have heard. You can stay or go.

This stays in your mind, but you do not imagine it make sense to do anything about it. Your mother would be heartbroken if you left. Your brothers and sisters would miss you. And you would miss them. And if you stay? More of the same things you are experiencing now.

More days, and more things happen. Perhaps you see someone who looks rather ordinary, buying supplies, and someone tells you that person is a member of the militia. You look more closely at the person, and they look less ordinary, and rather determined and brave. Perhaps someone from the militia has heard that you might be interested, or has not heard, but just wants to talk with people of your age. They meet you and tell you the same things you already knew. They fight for the people. They mean no one any harm. They uphold the dignity of the

people—your people. There are many ways you can help. You can come to the training and find out. Here is how you get to the camp. You will find others your age. And everyday you witness more insults and small disrespectful acts by the government, the soldiers, the police. They are hard to take.

One day you just decide to do it. There might not be anything about this day that is any different from one hundred other days. It is just *the* day. You walk out of your house and you do not act any different from usual. You meet a friend, and you and your friend start off walking. It is a very long walk. You are hungry. You cannot go on the streets for most of the way because the soldiers know where the camp is and they will know what you are doing, and they will stop you if they see you. They might even detain you or worse. This has been planned, but it is harder than it seemed. Then, you see someone with a rifle, and it is not a regular soldier. The person you see approaches you, and you are afraid, paralyzed. You tell them you have come to join up. You are glad you look young now, too young to be a soldier in disguise. Then there are two, and one of them is a girl. They look serious as they tell you to empty your pockets. One pats you all over to be sure you have no weapons. They do not talk to one another or to you, except to tell you what to do. They are busy. They have things to do. They are working together. It looks as if they have done this before. The other holds the rifle just in case. They find out you are unarmed. They walk with you the rest of the way, and then you are at camp, and you are about to become a member of the militia, to free your people and you know you might be hurt, but you also do not think so. Not yet. And you can always change your mind. The camp is impressive. You are scared and excited, and you cannot really separate the two.

Credible?

From all that we have read, all we have learned, all we have been told and witnessed for ourselves, this seems like a credible story of the development of a child soldier, who might volunteer for a militia. Once in the militia, this soldier might be persuaded to become a member of an elite suicide squad.

CHAPTER 5

MOST VICTIMS OF WAR ARE CIVILIANS

Victims of Twenty-First Century War: Are We All in This Together?

War, as Herbert Hoover, is reported to have said, is declared by older men, but it is the youth who must fight and die.[1] Perhaps today we should say that it is young men and women who carry out the wars, and anyone—or everyone—might die. For whether it is a paramilitary attacking a crowd that includes government officials, terrorists attacking civilians, or an overt, declared war using the most sophisticated technology available, the attacks are carried out, for the most part, by young men and women. And, in sheer numbers, the victims are more often civilians than government officials or soldiers (Burnham *et al.* 2004).[2] And should all our preventive efforts fail, and a nuclear attack occurs, whether it is launched by terrorists or by a recognized government, many, many civilians will die. Should a nuclear war begin, almost all of us may, in fact, die.

Youth in war-affected areas are only too aware of the costs of war to civilians, as so many of them have lost parents, sisters, brothers, cousins, and friends. Youth around the world, moreover, are aware that the ultimate war—a nuclear war—is possible, and that awareness, though not always front and center, affects everything.

Costs of War: Young Men and Women

A great deal is known about the losses our young adult generation is suffering in the long Iraq war. It seems safe to conclude, based on various reports, that field medicine has improved to the point that many military personnel who might have died in previous wars are surviving today. But some of those who survive have severe and disabling injuries and many with or without physical injuries have disabling

mental health problems (estimates for significant mental health problems are around 30 percent). Thus we have a generation of young American veterans—caring, altruistic young men and women, who were willing to go into harm's way to serve their country in the hopes that by risking their own lives they could protect their families and friends back home. Many of them, as well as the families and friends they wanted to protect, will bear the burdens of war for the rest of their lives. There has been a high rate of suicide and a high rate of homicide among American veterans of the Iraq war. Even those who are resilient and can return, without disabling injuries, to the families they left, return bearing the cost of witnessing the horrors of war. They need time and support to readjust. War is costly in personal terms. As writer Jose Narosky put it, "In war there are no unwounded soldiers."[3]

Young American and coalition soldiers have been involved in mortal danger, and have seen their comrades die. Their collective personal experience of death, suffering, loss, and of harming and killing others, parallels the experience of young soldiers around the world and throughout history, including those who were forced to fight and those who volunteered, and including those who fought with a regular military and those with a rebel group. Their mothers and fathers feel the same fears, dread, losses, and rage at the enemy that the families of young soldiers around the world feel. American Gold Star mothers,[4] who would give anything and everything to never have had that designation, nevertheless are honored by their communities, and there is an eerie parallel to the honors bestowed on the families who have sent sons and daughters to combat the world over, including the mothers of our adversaries and the mothers of our allies. Some would argue that the same anguished feelings are experienced by the mothers of those young men and women who, in their own minds, misguided as those minds might be, chose to be martyrs in the cause of bringing their people's plight to attention through dramatic, violent attacks. They would point out that even if those mothers may pretend to be happy, they only act happy and proud. For they and other members of their family might be perceived as less loyal to the cause if they appeared sad, and would therefore be at grave risk if they showed their tears. Viewed that way, one might have some compassion for a mother who has lost a child and must hide her grief and shame in order to save the lives of the rest of her family.

Some might recoil in horror at any comparison between the mother of a soldier and the mother of a terrorist, no matter what the motivation of the misguided terrorist might have been, and no matter how the mother's heart may ache. While we do not, in any sense, think these two are equivalent or identical, we do think that it is critical to examine whether there is any common ground that can lead to common understanding. The twenty-first-century world is small and our fates are more closely intertwined than ever before. We will never be able to end terrorism through increased violence. The first task we have is to understand, as well as we can, the hearts and minds of those misguided children who would be terrorists and of their parents.

In order to prevent terrorism, we must truly understand the mind-set and experiences of child soldiers, including those involved in terrorist actions, and those who might in the future be involved in a terrorist act in which they plan to die, we must search deeply for any way to connect with those experiences, and for any way that their experiences are parallel to those we know. We must also try to understand not only how we see child soldiers and their families, but also how they see themselves and their world. The knowledge thus gained, which is not the same as agreeing with others or endorsing their beliefs or actions, is critical to preventing terrorism and war. The distinguished psychologist Ralph White said "Em-pathy can help two or more nations avoid the dangers of misperception that lead to the wars most would prefer not to fight in the first place" (2004). We will not be able to win the war for hearts and minds if we do not understand, and cannot identify with, the hearts and minds of our adversaries, as well as the hearts and minds of our allies.

Military Service versus Rebel Militia

Some would argue that even if the families and friends of young American soldiers suffer the same way the families and friends of young child soldiers do, and even if the young American soldiers, as well as child soldiers from terrorist organizations, kill enemies and watch their friends die, and even if the greatest number of victims of war in any war are civilians, there is still a fundamental difference between American soldiers on the one hand, and youth in militia who engage in terrorist actions on the other. Most would say that our soldiers do not set out to kill innocent civilians, or noncombatants, and that while there is some risk to any civilian in a war zone, the civilians are not the targets of our soldiers. They might add that our soldiers do not seek to cause terror. Some would say that our soldiers are only fighting because our country was under attack.

Given the accuracy of all that, the experiences of twenty-first-century young American soldiers and the experiences of child soldiers in rebel militia still have much in common. American soldiers returning from twenty-first-century wars might remind the older generation of the complexities and gray areas of modern wars. The "enemies" in these wars are not only adults in uniform; anyone could be an enemy, no matter how innocent they look. Some soldiers have been ordered to kill civilians who appear to pose an imminent threat, only to find that they had posed no threat at all. Some have killed people posing as civilians who, it turns out, would have killed them and their comrades had they had a chance. And some have been killed by persons who looked, for all the world, like allies. Some have killed civilians as part of a larger campaign to do away with enemies who hid themselves among civilians in order to be harder to find. Some have been the targets of attacks by invisible civilian enemies who plant improvised explosive devices and then leave the devices to explode and destroy American

troops. Many of our soldiers have seen young children die. In some fundamental, internal, psychological, and spiritual way, these young Americans share a horrifying set of experiences with young soldiers around the world, and, although there are some fundamental differences, they also share these experiences with children who volunteer, and with children who are coerced, into militias.

Some of our young soldiers share something else in common with child soldiers in other parts of the world: they are members of minority ethnic and racial groups that have suffered indignities, frustrations, limited opportunities, and violations of their civil rights in their home communities. In the military, many have found a shared identity within a more diverse, more cohesive, more fair, and merit-based organization. However, for our American youth, the occupation of soldier, and the status of veteran, will, presumably, increase their standing in their communities, and in the society at large. It will provide them advantages in the areas of education, civil service jobs, and health care. These benefits are not likely to be forthcoming to child soldiers around the world. Indeed, when child soldiers who have been coerced, or who have volunteered, to be part of a militia in many parts of the world, escape or are rescued, or leave the militia, their families do not always want them to come back. The families may see them as being dangerous, or they may know that the family will be at risk because of their former status. That is, they know that their children may still have enemies from their own, or from opposition forces. Those enemies may attack them and may also attack members of their families. The families of former child soldiers may, in fact, fear them because they have become, in their eyes, trained killers, and fear the effects on their other children of being associated with them.

Parents of Youthful Terrorists Who Have Died in Attacks

A key question asked by many Americans, including professionals, about child terrorists who die in an attack, is how can their parents be proud of them, or at least act proud of them? How can they sometimes be seen celebrating? How do the parents of youthful terrorists, who do not have the opportunity to decide whether to welcome them home, explain their childrens' planned deaths, and the killing of civilians that are associated with those deaths? As we noted earlier, some of those parents are simply pretending to be proud. Yet what of those who may be actually proud? Surely the parents and communities do not simply say that their children were heroes because they committed heinous acts of violence against innocent civilians. They do not celebrate their children because the children have committed monstrous acts. Either they are only pretending to be proud, or, in their minds the actions of their children are at least justified, if not virtuous. Their points of view about what their children have done may differ from ours in some radical way that enables them to think that their sons and daughters acted in pro-social, altruistic ways. Or they may be heartbroken

and feel betrayed by those who recruited their child, and yet be afraid to show it. We conclude that either of these is possible, and probably each accounts for some parental reactions. That is, some parents are probably proud, and believe that their children acted heroically. That is not so hard to believe when we consider families whose rights have been violated, who perhaps have had other children killed, kidnapped, or raped by government forces. Perhaps the parents themselves would have been inclined to seek revenge, but could not afford to do so, because their other children needed their care. Perhaps, in their view, misguided as that view might be, the child who died in an attack in some way did what had to be done—in some way showed the government that they could not continue to oppress their people and do so with impunity. That they could not rape their daughters, kidnap their sons, and attack their villages and not have to answer for it. For those who live in societies where there is no viable legal infrastructure, or where it is only available for those who can pay a high price or who have connections, perhaps this is perceived as the only way to fight back. While this is not, in our opinion, an optimal response, it is, in our opinion, an understandable response by parents. In some peculiar way, it even may be seen as understandable by those who have felt that their government betrayed or abandoned them in an hour of need, and who felt they had no recourse.

Chain of Events

When we see only the final event in a chain of events—a child detonating a bomb that blows up the child and people we believe to be innocent bystanders, we only have one tiny bit of the story. As noted by Moghaddam (2006), Horgan (2005), and others, becoming a terrorist is a process in which each step taken makes the next step seem more normal and less outlandish. Moreover, these steps can be described and documented. The likelihood that a child will embark on the steps that begin this process by voluntarily joining an organization that engages in terrorism is influenced by their families and the immediate circumstances of their families, villages, friends, and neighbors. But it is also influenced by their government, by their culture, by their history, and by their understanding of regional and global concerns.

The immediate decision to join a militia may be, for some, the result of a particularly terrible thing that happened to them or to a family member or friend at the hands of the dominant group that the militia they join is fighting. For others, it may be just one too many small things. For still others, a personal desire to belong, or a felt need to get away from home, or other personal reasons. For still others it may be a proactive altruistic desire to help their community. Once in the group, some find the group support, mentoring, adequacy of basic resources, disciplined training, and shared mission appealing. (Veterans of regular government-sponsored military and those who know veterans, may see some

parallels between these experiences of youth in militias and youth serving with recognized military groups. That is, the mentoring, camaraderie, shared mission, disciplined training, and so on are sources of pride and gratification to regular military as well as to soldiers in rebel groups.) Some young women in militia find the experience of equal treatment with young men to be gratifying—again, not totally unlike women in regular military groups.

Creating Martyrs: What Americans Need to Know

We set out to understand how youth become involved in violent acts in which they planfully and intentionally die. We thought that there might be some common themes in the families, communities, and societies where they grow up, and we found that some combination of experiences of indignity, closely witnessing loss and suffering, unfairness, uncertainty about the future, limited hope, coercion, recruitment, lack of trust in the government that is considered by the international community to be legitimate, awareness of unfairness in international events, altruism, and a misguided belief that dying in an attack will improve the conditions of one's people, are common elements. We also came to believe that awareness of the existence of nuclear weapons, and of the possibility of nuclear disaster, influences children who become terrorists and their families, as much as it influences all families and children all over the world. We cannot say with certainty exactly how awareness of the possibility of nuclear disaster translates into an added element in the decisions by children who become terrorists, but we can say with some certainty that the possibility of a meaningless death looms large when one considers a nuclear attack. This may, for example, make planned death less unthinkable. It may make death with meaning more appealing, since a meaningless death is contemplated. We do not think that the existence of nuclear weapons, or the possibility of their use in an unexpected attack, is likely to be the sole or major reason why a reasonably healthy young person would join a militia, but we do think it forms a part of the background for everyone, including youth making decisions about the value of life and the certainty of life. No matter what else we may think about it, the possibility of nuclear war puts us all in the same boat.

Common American Theories About Youthful Terrorists

Most Americans ultimately assume that any decision to perform a terrorist act is so foreign and so outlandish that it cannot be understood within our frame of reference at all. But before Americans throw up our hands in despair, we try to find a way to understand these strange actions. First, Americans tend to consider the children and imagine that they must all be mentally ill—depressed or suicidal to begin with. Perhaps this terrorist act in which they planfully die is just a

convenient way to do what they wanted to do anyway. Perhaps they have simply decided to take others along with them to death. Then they look at the parents and assume that the parents are either mentally ill, or do not love their children. For if they are sane and loving, how could they allow this to happen? When Americans see media coverage suggesting that the families celebrate or feel proud of their dead child, they think the parents are detached, uncaring, and lacking in moral values. How could they be proud of a child who committed mass murder? With encouragement from the media, many parents only consider Palestinian terrorists when they think about children who die in an attack. They go on to assume that there is something about the religion of Islam that is so strange and crazy that it fosters outrageous acts like terrorism in which youth blow themselves up, and it fosters parental pride in those actions. But the majority of the world's child terrorists are not Islamic jihadists, and do not identify with Islam at all.

Still there are two major impediments to understanding child terrorists: First, all those sincere, if desperate, attempts to understand, often take place just after an attack, when the American parents are not fully able to focus their best cognitive skills on the problem, because the very idea of a child killing unsuspecting civilians and dying intentionally in an attack is so horrifying that it compromises our ability to be detached and reasonable. Furthermore, Americans have limited knowledge about other cultures, and about how it is to live in situations with severe restrictions of civil rights, and common violations of human rights. That, of course, makes it harder to understand.

Radical Differences in Experience

Most Americans have always assumed that, with a few allowances for poverty, lack of education, food and music preferences, language differences, and the experiences typical of rural life, people all over the world are pretty much like Americans. To the extent that they are not like Americans, we tend to believe that they are deficient—possibly because of lack of education—backward, or blocked in their attempts at progress. We also make an even more serious blunder: we tend to assume that they would like to be like us, and that they see us as fundamentally good people, with a fundamentally good system.

These assumptions are made by even the best-educated among us. We know this because our colleagues in the field of psychology, who, arguably, have the greatest motivation to understand the similarities and differences among people, now struggle to expand their previously very narrowly defined concept of how people are and how they should be. It is very hard for mainstream Americans to see differences between Americans and those of other countries as anything other than deficiencies or problems on the part of the others. There is a reason for this. We have been the most dominant people in the most dominant country

on earth, and we have not had to understand or accept others, much less see them as our equals in any way.

Underscoring the Need for Better Knowledge of the World

It became painfully evident after the September 11 attacks that, despite the ideal of a free press, and despite unprecedented access to international news via the Internet, many Americans were woefully ignorant of world affairs. Sadly, in 2008, the lack of knowledge that became evident in 2001 does not seem to have been successfully addressed, and it continues to spawn many jokes made about Americans' ignorance of geography and international political affairs.[5,6] If actions on the international stage are to be influenced by a knowledgeable electorate acting through its representatives, the ordinary educated citizen needs to know more about the world outside the United States.[7]

Lack of awareness of history, geography, and international affairs results in serious limitations when even well-educated Americans try to understand how young people could be engaged in terrorism, for they seldom consider multiple layers of influence. For example, if an American parent is trying to understand why a Sri Lankan youth engaged in a terrorist attack in which he planfully died, it is unlikely that the American would understand factors such as the history of occupation of Sri Lanka, the history of favoritism shown by British occupiers, earlier youth rebellions, contemporary human rights violations, religious differences, and so on. Even at professional conferences, most conferees who have not engaged in indepth study of terrorism ask only a few questions about youth engaged in terrorist actions: How could they (the children) do that? How could their parents let them do that? How could their parents possibly be proud of them for doing that? The actual answers to those questions will require knowledge of the local, country, and international politics, and global realities affecting the children, as well as cultural traditions, patterns, and expectations. Without that knowledge, it will seem quite hopeless for the United States to intervene at a preventative level and we will be left with the conclusion that the only solution imaginable is to kill or detain enough terrorists that the threat would be reduced. This of course turns out to be folly, since for every terrorist killed or detained by the United States, many youth became easier to recruit, and the numbers of potential terrorists grows. A radically different approach is needed.

Ecological Psychology

Ecological psychology, developed by the late Dr. Urie Bronfenbrenner and his colleagues, provides a helpful model of influence on children that includes family, school (for those children lucky enough to attend school), neighborhood, community, country, and even the international community. In this model, often

represented by concentric circles with the child in the center, each circle is influenced by every other circle, and the influence is mutual. While the family influences the child, the child also influences the family. The family influences the neighborhood and community, as well as being influenced by them. A model such as this, rather than a narrow model that looks only at the child and family for reasons why a child becomes a terrorist, is needed. At the outer edge of this model is the entire international community. In most cases, of course, one child does not have much influence on the regional or international community. But the international community, as we have seen and shall see, has a great deal of influence on the child. Moreover, it is possible for a child who becomes engaged in a terrorist action to influence the family, community, country, and even the international community. It is our understanding that something like this possibility sometimes adds to the appeal of joining a militia. In the trailer for *My Daughter the Terrorist*,[8] a translation of one of the female Black Tigers (those training for missions that will lead to their deaths) reflects proud awareness that one terrorist can have quite a large impact. For children who think that they are doing something virtuous, a large impact has an even greater appeal.

A Very "Good Cause"

When we asked some children and some older adults in Sri Lanka to tell us the minimum age they thought made sense for entering a fighting force, the average age given by adults was nineteen, while the average given by children was eighteen and a half. However, when we asked whether, if it were a "very good cause," it would be justified for younger children to fight, every adult said the minimum age would be the same, whatever the cause. The average age provided by children, however, dropped to just a little over sixteen years. This suggests that indeed youth might be vulnerable to persuasion by a recruiter when it comes to signing up to fight if the recruiter can only convince them that it is a good cause. There is a parallel with the tactics widely believed to be used by Palestinian recruiters looking for ordinary devout young men and women to engage in what the young men and women see as martyrdom. The recruiters convince them that it is a very good cause. It seems likely that some of the parents of these children, too, think that the cause they are fighting for is a very good cause.

A Very Good Cause: What Do They Know and How Do They Know It?

Most child soldiers and child terrorists live in areas of their country where literacy rates are not high, and many people in the older generation, especially women, have not been well-educated and do not read well; some do not read at all. (Literacy rates in Sri Lanka vary by area of the country. While the overall rate

is about 90 percent, according to UNESCO, some areas have rates of about 60 percent.)[9] Furthermore, circumstances do not favor a free press, and this makes it unlikely that citizens, especially those not in the dominant group, will believe in official news reports. In Sri Lanka, for example, many do not feel they can believe what they read from official sources, and their skepticism is well-placed. In an article on a recent attack in Sri Lanka, the *New York Times* noted the difficulty of getting the true story. "Both sides regularly make conflicting claims. Their reports are impossible to verify because Nordic monitors who had been keeping watch over a shaky cease-fire left the island in January."[10] Furthermore, in Sri Lanka, the government has been accused in the disappearances of key journalists in war-affected areas, further increasing doubt about the government's interest in a free press. A recent report from the organization called Reporters Without Borders stated, "Sri Lanka holds the record for the greatest number of disappearances reported to the UN. Among them are two Jaffna journalists: Subramaniam Ramachandran, a journalist on *Thinakural,* who has not been seen since February after being arrested by the army; and Vadivel Nimalarajah, a sub editor on *Uthayan,* who was abducted from the street, after spending the night working at his office."[11]

As a result of difficulties getting accurate reports, people in countries affected by internal wars are likely to make their own decisions about what to believe, and are more likely to believe what they are told by their trusted friends, neighbors, and family members than what is published in newspapers or broadcast on the radio. In countries where human rights can be violated with impunity, and where the governing body is not seen as friendly, there is a level of suspicion that is in some ways healthy and in others problematic. Governments everywhere, of course, are believed to spin stories to their own advantage, but where there is no free press, and not even a semblance of a free press, and no functional legal infrastructure where a free and fair trial can be anticipated, what is published is only seen as valuable for its reflection of what the government wants people to believe. Indeed, to some degree every story is suspect. Unfortunately, those who cannot believe what the official news sources publish are potentially at the mercy of the most persuasive and charismatic people they meet. In some cases, these might be teachers, clergy, or educated people of good will who have the best interest of the people at heart, and who try to provide a balanced and rational approach. In others, however, they may be people with an agenda of their own, who inspire their listeners to do what they want them to do by bending the truth, by exaggerating, or by lying.

Trust and Distrust in the United States

In the United States, despite the principle of a free press, many believe that there are some problems with the press in that (1) various networks are

considered to have political leanings, and (2) networks are considered to be too centralized, and too likely to be influenced by corporate, rather than citizen, interests. Despite this, however, in the United States and other stable democracies, the history and ideal of a free press, along with a legal infrastructure that helps protect freedom of speech, affords some degree of assurance that the whole story will, sooner or later, be available. Furthermore, continued interest in a free press, together with widely available access to high-speed Internet through libraries and educational institutions, as well as many homes, enables people who seek them to get a variety of viewpoints, including some from international sources. It would be very difficult for the government to control news sources completely.

Still, even in the United States, some who think of themselves as nonmainstream, whether because of their religious or political leanings, or because they are immigrants or members of minority groups, also have a healthy suspicion of news reports, based on multiple experiences where members of their identity group were wrongly accused, and wrongly portrayed. Many still prefer to rely on trusted members of their own communities for news and trustworthy interpretation of news. Furthermore, psychologists have shown that people of all backgrounds have a tendency, when stressed or afraid, to emphasize insider/outsider distinctions. If you do not identify with the officials of your country, you will not expect them to have your best interest at heart. You will be even more inclined, in such situations, to listen to and believe those with whom you identify, rather than with official news sources. The burgeoning of news Web sites for people of various political and religious groups, including conservatives and fundamentalist Christians, left-leaning progressives, environmentalists, and so on, is evidence of this principle being played out. In the United States, the principle of a free press, and the legal infrastructure to defend it, helps mitigate and limit the impact of bias in the news media. Nevertheless, youth in the United States, like youth everywhere, are subject to persuasive and charismatic leaders who offer their own interpretation of world events.

How Distrust of News Contributes to Recruitment of Children in War-Affected Areas

Imagine, for a moment, a teenager in a war-affected country, who has seen the horrors of war, who has known people who have disappeared, who has perhaps been displaced, lived in refugee camps, known of violations by soldiers, and who does not believe the government-sponsored news media. Now imagine a recruiter who is looking for youth to persuade to join their opposition militia. Imagine how vulnerable the teenager might be to recruitment. The recruiter might, for example, convince the teenager, or group of teenagers, that he or she—the recruiter—is one of "them"—a member of their own group. As such, his version of the story is apt to be seen as more credible than that of the

government. One can imagine, for example, a recruiter describing exaggerations of actual human rights violations, or generating such rage, fear, and hopelessness that children begin to believe that the only possible way to effect change is to join a militia, that the militia is fighting for a good cause, and that the only way to stop the government abuses and thus protect their families and loved ones is to mount an unexpected attack, and the only way to do that is if the young recruit is willing to die for this cause.

This recruitment strategy may also be used in the EU or the United States, where immigrants, or the children of immigrants, may have been subject to bias and stereotyping and therefore distrust the official news sources. They may be at risk of persuasion by sources they consider to be of their own people—whatever identity group that may be, whether religious, ethnic, racial, or national. The recruiters may use the youth's own experience of stereotyping and bias, together with the youth's larger identity group's status as victims of unfair treatment, and stir up youthful hate and an inclination toward revenge, or stir up a sense that only violence can effect change. Youthful idealism, combined with such misinformation, can lead young people to believe that only their own willingness to die can save their people.

For many children in war-affected areas, however, perhaps especially those with the benefit of an education, challenges to obtaining news do not prevent them from being aware of national and international circumstances affecting them.

"Stop Providing Weapons"

We wanted to know whether the children we met in Sri Lanka thought other countries could help to end the war. We knew from their answers to earlier questions that the children were well aware that aid groups from many countries, including the United States, had provided assistance to their island after the tsunami. When we asked how these same countries might help end the war, we got some expected—and some unexpected—responses. Some saw the United States as possibly playing a mediating role, telling each side to work with the other and stop fighting, for example. Others said they did not think anyone from outside the island could help. But some of the children surprised us by saying that if the United States wanted to help, it should stop providing weapons to the Sri Lankan government. This was in June 2007, and we were embarrassed that we had not thought about whether the United States was supplying military aid to the Sri Lankan government. Indeed, we learned that it was. Subsequently, however, the United States has severely cut military aid to Sri Lanka. Their stated goal in cutting the aid was not directly to end the war; however, the United States does want to pressure the Sri Lankan government to improve their record on human rights.[12]

With the children's unexpected responses, we realized that we, like many other researchers on child soldiers and child terrorists, had simply not recognized the role

that awareness of international affairs plays in the lives of children in war-affected areas. Eventually, we became convinced that if we thought we had the answers to why children become terrorists by examining only the everyday lives of the children, and their concerns about the local situation of their families and neighbors, we would be missing an important set of factors in youthful decision-making. We have since had many conversations with colleagues who have been engaged in international research and international negotiations. We conclude that we cannot leave the subject of what brings children to terrorism without exploring global considerations, including past, present, and possible future global circumstances, as they are likely to be viewed by youth from war-affected areas. Those global considerations include the uneven distribution of resources and power, which appears to many as greed by wealthy countries; the history of colonialism and fear of neocolonialism; perceptions of the failure of the Western world to recognize violations of human rights or other indignities in their countries; and—in the background—awareness of the threat of nuclear war.

Resources

We have no doubt that poor youth in Sri Lanka and most other countries where youth are involved in militias and terrorist activities are aware that the average American, and the average European, have more resources than most of the people in their countries, and that Western countries use their resources to influence world events. The countries that are home to most child soldiers and youthful terrorists, like most countries, have histories of colonial rule. The use of power by wealthy countries to influence events in their countries (such as by providing military aid) must have some echoes of that past.

We also think it is safe to assume that child soldiers in Sri Lanka and other countries are aware that many nations have nuclear weapons. Sri Lanka, at its closest point, for example, is just eighteen miles from India, a nuclear power. However, we do not yet know how youth in these countries interpret what they know, nor do we know how accurate their knowledge may be.

While children in war-affected areas are likely to know quite a bit about the United States. I doubt that one in a thousand American youth, or one in a hundred American adults, knows much about the history or current circumstances in any of the twenty-seven countries where, according to Wessells (2006, p. 10), there were children involved in armed conflict between 2001 and 2004, such as Sri Lanka, Uganda, Colombia, Cameroon, Afghanistan, Nepal, Sudan, Rwanda, Angola, India, and Indonesia. It seems even less likely that they would know the names of the affected groups, their leaders, or of the existence of war. Americans in recent years have not felt the need to know. The United States has been very important to the people of those countries, but, up until now, the people of those countries have not seemed as important to Americans.

"Do not Discount Our Generation"

Recently, a student in one of my classes took the older generation to task for not recognizing how acutely aware her generation of American students is when it comes to the costs of terrorism and counterterrorism. She said, "Most of us either have friends now, or have lost a friend, in Iraq or Afghanistan. People in your generation assume we don't understand or think about it. But we do. Don't discount our generation." This American student, along with contemporary youth the world over, in fact, face multiple, potentially deadly, challenges: terrorism, nuclear catastrophe, (whether initiated by legitimate governments or other groups), urgent environmental concerns, violence in institutions, danger of global economic recession, and war are some of the challenges that come to mind. Youth in America, like their parents, saw the events of September 11, 2001, unfold. Like their parents, they continue to fear the next terrorist attack, and that fear affects their behavior. But unlike their parents, they know that their generation is bearing the greatest losses associated with twenty-first-century wars. They face an uncertain future, with difficulties and losses associated with both terrorism and by counterterrorist efforts.[13] They are aware that the entire future of civilization is uncertain, due to the existence of nuclear weapons and the possibility they will be used in a reckless, unanticipated manner. For while it seems unlikely that Russia or other countries known to have nuclear capability would begin a nuclear war without any warning, and without an escalating conflict that might provide time to avert a global disaster, a terrorist group that obtained such a weapon could be expected to use it without warning, in order to provoke panic and destabilize society. Despite the fact that such use would seem to violate the idea that terrorists want lots of people watching, rather than lots of people dead[14] there is reason to believe that al Qaeda, at least, is interested in using a nuclear weapon. Although experts have seen this danger ahead for some time, most of us were unaware of the high risk of a nonstate entity using nuclear weapons, and most of us felt that it was likely that the scenario of mutually assured-destruction lead to fairly reliable deterrence. Most Americans learned about the terrorist threat in the aftermath of September 11. This, then, is the first generation to live with fear of sudden unanticipated, unexplained nuclear catastrophe. (At the end of this chapter there is a section explaining the current nuclear threat, along with a reference to a longer work on the history of nuclear threat.)

Shared Future: Human Rights, Terrorism, and Youth Around the World

The United Nations has a simple dividing line between child soldiers (which it, and other bodies, discourage) and adult soldiers: age 18. Since the United Nations had to draw some sort of line, and most youth are fairly strong and physically fairly

mature at eighteen, the choice is understandable, although it is somewhat arbitrary. Having worked with young college students, we cannot help asking ourselves whether eighteen-year-old soldiers are really much better able to manage the extreme stresses of war than sixteen- or seventeen-year olds. The arbitrary use of chronological age at all, whether eighteen or any other age, is puzzling as a cutoff point to leaders in some of areas where the United Nations is encouraging its acceptance. In some areas, sexual maturity, for example, has been the designated sign of adulthood. And even though eighteen years old is consistent with legal adult status in the United States, neuropsychologists and developmental psychologists would not see it as an obvious dividing point between child and adult, and in fact they might prefer an older age—say twenty-five—when judgment and decision-making processes are more mature. We wonder, too, whether the current generation of youth is, indeed, experiencing war differently from past generations. While past generations typically fought wars where survival was uncertain, most of the time the enemy was somewhat clearly defined or definable. By contrast, awareness of loosely defined, ever-changing terrorist groups permeates global politics and war in 2008. It is hard to know whether the person who appears to be your local ally is indeed an ally, whether the area secured today will be secure tomorrow, and whether the people who appear to most need help are part of a trap.

Nuclear Taboo

Once we came to the realization that children who become terrorists probably have some awareness, however accurate or inaccurate, about the threat of nuclear disaster, we reluctantly realized that our work would be incomplete if we did not include information about the real threat of nuclear weapon use. Child terrorism is not a cheery topic, but the information in this chapter is the least cheery of all. We know from work of colleague Steve Zeitlin, cited earlier, that for many people the nuclear threat is a taboo subject. We did not expect to have to learn as much as we did about it, and we sometimes felt reluctant to think about when the information came our way. Yet we became quite convinced that youth, as well as adults, all over the world are at least dimly aware of the threat of nuclear attack and the threat of nuclear catastrophe, and we believe that, directly or indirectly, it affects the choices they make, the actions they engage in, and the value they place on their own, and others' lives. While we do not think that child soldiers or child terrorists think about nuclear weapons consciously everyday, we do strongly believe that they, like other children around the world, live in an atmosphere where one of the important elements of reality is the threat of nuclear disaster.

The children we talked to in Sri Lanka, who had witnessed a disaster a couple of years earlier, when the tsunami brought destruction to much of the island, told us that they thought a great deal about the possibility of another tsunami. They said they tried to distract themselves by praying and by thinking about other

things, and that they also had specific escape plans. (All of this was, evidently, known only to their peers.) They were quite successful in coping with the fear, but they told us that at night, when all was quiet, they sometimes thought about the possibility of another tsunami. It seems likely to us that the threat of nuclear attack is less immediate, less real, and more dim, but nevertheless it is there in a way parallel to the threat of a tsunami. Most of the time, when children and adults are busy with other things, the threat of nuclear attack is out of mind. Yet it is not completely inaccessible. Like the threat of environmental disaster, drought, flood, or a terrorist attack, the threat of nuclear attack or nuclear accident are like an unpleasant noise or scent; we habituate, but we are on the verge of awareness, nevertheless.

With that in mind, we realized we could not provide a thorough analysis of what makes children decide to join militia or engage in terrorist acts, including those in which they die, without considering the threat of nuclear attacks, a threat that makes uncertainty and the potential for terror a normal part of the mental landscape.

Very Brief Historical Overview

Those of us in the older generation in the United States remember air raid drills and bomb shelters as quirky symbols of the 1950s. The 1950s also, nostalgically, are recalled as an era of economic growth and of a return to what we thought would be a stable new normalcy. Middle class American children at that time were only dimly aware of the grueling and frightening sequence of world events of the recent past, including economic depression; genocide; an attack on the United States at Pearl Harbor; internment camps where American citizens of Japanese descent were detained; a terrible international war, fought mostly in Europe, with horrendous civilian and military losses on all sides; the race to develop a nuclear weapon, followed by the unfathomable suffering resulting aftermath of its use. While many Americans were readjusting to life as families with fathers present, scientists, world leaders, and others more prescient than most were realizing that this new era, with nuclear weapons available, might be the beginning of the end of civilization as we knew it. Albert Einstein, for one, was distressed—possibly tortured is not too strong a word—by the thought that science had now unleashed the power to destroy all of mankind. He believed it was only a matter of time before a nuclear war occurred, unless nations agreed to cooperate in what he thought was the only way to avert it: through the establishment of a strong international governing body, capable of enforcement. He was envisioning something stronger than the United Nations, but with many of its components (Nathan and Norden 1960).

The threat of nuclear catastrophe has gone from central focus to just barely being in public awareness in the United States, and back again to central focus

at several points between the 1950s and the current time. Notably in the 1980s, there was strong international awareness of the nuclear threat. Women, in particular, in the United States, did quite a lot to bring this threat to public attention, and to protest for disarmament. A group called Women's Action for Nuclear Disarmament,[15] along with several others, had a strong presence.[16] However, whether, at any given moment, the real potential of humans to set in motion an unstoppable sequence of events that will inevitably lead to the end of our entire civilization in a matter of moments was central or peripheral in focus, it has been a tremendous force in human society over the last half century. We cannot ignore or neglect its impact on any generation, including youth, in any part of the world.

Contemporary Nuclear Threat

The nuclear threat is central in focus now with the possibility of nonstate entities obtaining and using a nuclear weapon. At an earlier period, the concept of mutually assured destruction as a deterrent was somewhat comforting, particularly when only the United States and the USSR had nuclear capability. However, a new approach to deterrence is needed, since, should a terrorist network such as al Qaeda obtain a nuclear weapon and use it, it would be difficult for the country attacked to respond in kind, since al Qaeda is an organization with no headquarters and not one but many geographic locations, some known to international security experts, very likely many unknown—in short, there would be nowhere, and everywhere, to bomb. It would be virtually impossible to wipe out al Qaeda without destroying much of civilization.

Most of us, youth or adult, do not spend many of our waking hours paralyzed by fear of nuclear weapons. Surely, whether or not it is in focus, the threat affects our behavior and the decisions we make, in subtle and not-so-subtle ways. While we were preparing this chapter, and the threat was constantly in our awareness, we could watch ourselves make decisions and provide advice that reflected our heightened consciousness of the threat. Willingness to acknowledge the sometimes dim, sometimes clear threat of nuclear disaster can help understand another of the conditions that likely contribute to making some children willing to die in an attack on others, and others willing to risk death in actions that have even a remote possibility of reducing the threat of terrorism. This same nuclear threat can also, paradoxically, suggest an as yet barely perceptible path toward improved international collaboration.

Nuclear Threat

The last part of this chapter is a report on some scenarios and evidence for the possibility of a nuclear attack on the United States. No experts offer a guarantee—or

even a great deal of optimism, that we can, on our current course, avoid all nuclear attacks—in the United States or elsewhere—in the foreseeable future. For those interested in pursuing the topic of the global nuclear threat in depth, a longer work on the history and current state of international nuclear weapons threat by Pugwash, the Nobel Prize winning organization of scientists who are working to prevent nuclear disaster, is available online. The longer work is called *Addressing the Nuclear Weapons Threat: The Russell–Einstein Manifesto, Fifty Years On* (Boutwell 2005).[17] We can imagine that, even without the deterrent of mutually assured destruction between or among groups that have nuclear power, citizens from around the world might unite to signal those in power that detonating such a weapon would be frowned upon by virtually everyone. This is likely to be a deterrent for most terrorist groups, who do not want to alienate their potential recruits. However, in order for such a signal to be conveyed, citizens will have to be aware of the potential for a nuclear attack.

Some Evidence and Scenarios for Possible Nuclear Attack on the United States

Harvard University Dean and Professor Graham Allison reported in his 2004 book, *Nuclear Terrorism,* that in October 2001 just weeks after the September 11, 2001 terrorist attacks on New York City, Washington DC, and Pennsylvania, the U.S. government received intelligence (that later turned out to be false) from an asset code named "Dragonfire" that terrorists had gotten a ten kiloton nuclear weapon into New York City. This incident was also discussed by former CIA Director, George Tenet, who wrote about it in his 2007 book, *At the Center of the Storm.* The weapon was reported to have been stolen from Russia following the dissolution of the former Soviet Union, and to have ended up in the hands of terrorists who were planning on using it in their next martyrdom mission.

Although it is now known that this intelligence was false, the government found it sufficiently credible that it dispatched NEST (Nuclear Emergency Support teams) teams to the city to locate and dismantle the weapon. President Bush began sending members of the government to secure locations outside of Washington DC for purposes of assuring continuity of government, in case a weapon had also been deployed to the capitol. The press subsequently began publishing stories about a "shadow government" that existed in case of a nuclear strike against the U.S. government. Had there been a bomb in downtown Manhattan, and had it been deployed, it would have killed millions instantly, and many more to come in the subsequent nuclear fallout. New York would become uninhabitable, and the economy of the United States would sustain a serious blow, if not collapse altogether.

According to Allison, this new intelligence was deemed at the time to be credible because of Osama bin Laden's long-standing interest in acquiring a nuclear

weapon. Allison reports that less than six months earlier, the U.S. government had received intelligence about "American Hiroshima" plans by al Qaeda to detonate a nuclear weapon on U.S. soil. (This was in reference to the nuclear weapons that were dropped on Hiroshima and Nagasaki Japan by the United States to end World War II.) Former CIA official and Head of the "Bin Laden Unit," Michael Scheuer (2004), reported that bin Laden sought and acquired religious approval from a Saudi Arabia Islamic cleric to use a nuclear weapon against the United States in retaliation for what bin Laden said was the murder of an estimated four million Muslims in recent history. In Scheuer's estimation, bin Laden did this specifically because he was criticized by the Islamic leadership following the September 11 attacks for not having obtained advance religious approval.

Although this specific intelligence from "Dragonfire" turned out to be false, the intent of al Qaeda and other terrorist organizations to acquire such weapons—or the material to assemble them—is thought to be real and substantial.

Regardless of whether or not nuclear weapons are now in the hands of terrorist organizations and/or on U.S. soil, it is, then, widely believed by credible sources that there is intent to acquire and use these weapons. Even though there have been no known terrorist attacks on U.S. soil since 9/11, many experts would argue that they are on the horizon and may at some point involve weapons of mass destruction, possibly nuclear weapons. With respect to predicting these attacks, Scheuer argues that bin Laden himself has been the most accurate predictor/reporter of attacks that follow in his frequent public statements. That is to say, when bin Laden has said in the past that he plans to attack, he follows through with these stated goals.

Following 9/11, Scheuer also reports, bin Laden was heavily criticized in the Islamic community for: (1) not acquiring religious approval for the attacks; and (2) not properly warning the United States and allowing its citizens to accept Allah prior to carrying out the operations. As if to address this proactively for the next set of attacks, Scheuer reports, bin Laden sought and acquired religious approval from a Saudi Arabian cleric in 2004 to kill four million Americans, the amount that has been estimated by bin Laden to have been killed by Western troops operating on the Arabian peninsula since 1991.

Could a Terrorist Organization Acquire a Nuclear Weapon?

According to reports in the media and by people such as Allison, acquiring a nuclear weapon may not be as far fetched as some would like to believe. As more and more countries around the globe have gone "nuclear," there exists an expanding number of potential resources open to terrorist organizations to acquire such weapons. For example, Allison reports that in 2001, al Qaeda met with two nuclear scientists from Pakistan's nuclear weapons program, both of whom worked under Dr. Abdul Qadeer Khan. Dr. Khan and these scientists are credited

with developing nuclear technology within the country of Pakistan, to be used for both energy and defense purposes. Such meetings are seen by some as cause for serious concern.

Another potential source of nuclear material and/or weapons is the former Soviet Union, which, when it officially dissolved, left questions about the security of its nuclear arsenal. In 1997 during a CBS *60 Minutes* interview, former Russian General Alexander Lebed told reporter Steve Kroft that the Russian government could not account for a significant number of Soviet suitcase nuclear weapons. General Lebed estimated the number to be roughly eighty-four, and went on to say that transporting such a weapon would be easy given its appearance (i.e., a suitcase) and detonating it would only take roughly twenty to thirty minutes. When asked where these weapons were, General Lebed could not answer the question as he did not know.

In October 2006, North Korea detonated their first nuclear weapon underground, and subsequently announced to the world that they had officially joined the elite league of nuclear nations. This poses significant risks to nations such as the United States. Despite a cease-fire between the nations signed over fifty years ago, they are still, technically, at war.

Could a Nuclear Weapon Be Transported into the United States?

The potential for transport of weapons across our border has been considered. A recent precedent for this kind of weapon delivery (although not nuclear weapons) occurred in 1999. Ahmed Ressam, an Algerian-born terrorist who had trained in one of Osama bin Laden's Afghanistan training camps, was apprehended with a car full of explosives as he attempted to enter the United States through the Port of Seattle. He was purportedly on his way to attack the Los Angeles airport (LAX).

There have also been discussions about the possibility that nuclear weapons or material might enter via shipping vessels. Given the extremely high number of containers coming in and out of the country each day, and the seeming impossibility of searching each one, this may be considered a viable way of transporting operatives and weapons into the country. Should a successful attack be carried out through this manner of transportation, there would be danger not only from the attack itself, but from the likely repercussions, including paralysis of segments of the shipping industry.

Overall, then, it is quite clear that those whose job it is to predict and prevent such attacks take the threat of a nuclear attack on the United States by a terrorist organization quite seriously.

CHAPTER 6

THE INVISIBLE GLOBAL NETWORK: ENVISIONING A NONVIOLENT PATH TO PEACE

The Fisherman

"You should bring your notebook. You might want to write something down." I grabbed my composition book while stepping out of the very hot van into the even hotter sun, and, following my guide, the young director of a local charity who served as translator for this part of my trip, I walked around and over traps and nets, across stone paths, and through pungent alleyways before getting to meet the Fisherman and his family. In these unusual circumstances, the translator and I had been mentoring and helping each other; I taught him all the psychology I could think of that might help him in his work; he taught me all he could about the island. He had decided that a visit with his friend, the Fisherman, would provide a perspective I had not heard before, and he was right.

In meetings in Sri Lanka, like many cultures that are less competitive and less impatient than mainstream America, one never enters into serious talk before tea and social conversation about the well-being of families and loved ones. In such cultures, one would never share important information with a complete stranger. On the other hand, once one has shared tea and such personal conversation, one is no longer a stranger. During the early phases of conversation, each participant judges the other, deciding how much to reveal and how much to keep to himself. In such cultures, if you are a friend of a friend, that helps, but your identity is tied to your family; they do not have to be famous or accomplished, but you must show that you and your family are close.

After serving us and engaging in gracious and friendly conversation about his family, and allowing me to speak of my family, the Fisherman settled in to talk about this important matter. He first told me that he is not an educated man, meaning that he has not spent much time in school. Such a statement of modesty

is characteristic in Sri Lanka and many other collectivist cultures. The focus is on the value of the group, rather than the individual. In such societies it is not seen as a virtue to stand out or to attract attention to oneself. Self-effacing talk and modesty are valued. He proceeded to talk about his views of the situation on the island, and what it is like to live in a war-affected country. "On the sea," he told me, "everyone from all ethnic groups gets together to fish, and there is no problem; only on land there are problems."[1] Here was something I had not heard before, nor had I considered, though it made perfect sense. On the water, with a shared purpose and shared risk, everyone must depend on each other. Differences must be put aside. And the identity with the fishing group becomes more important than the ethnic, religious, or regional identity that fuels ongoing conflict on land. This is the same principle that caused everyone on the island, no matter what ethnicity or religion, to cooperate just after the tsunami. By contrast, on land, a couple of years after the tsunami, neither tasks nor risks are shared across ethnic groups, and one's ethnic, religious, and/or regional identity, is reinforced by friends, neighbors, and family.

The Fisherman continued. His comments reflected a deep and well-considered awareness of the multiple ironies and contrasts of ongoing ethnic conflict. "After the tsunami, we learned to love each other, but because of unequal distribution of aid, we learned to hate each other." "We all got together [60 years ago] to request independence from the Queen...but after we achieved independence we did not share equally, and that was the disaster." "The armed groups...cannot imagine peace." Each of these contrasts reflects a well-known psychological principle. With shared purpose (seeking independence, seeking survival and recovery); shared risk (the tsunami, the occupying country); shared identity (victims of a disaster, victims of a colonizer), we pay less attention to differences. When we focus on shared identity, our identities as adversaries fade. It also suggested a principle put forward by several social scientists: Terrorism, in its essence, is less about religion, ethnicity, or poverty, than it is about fairness, human rights, and resources. Conflicting ethnic and religious identities are the basis of terrorism because they are the basis of violations of civil rights. These identities may continue strong, but they will not be the basis of conflict when they are not the basis of unfair distribution of resources.

Neither civilian occupational identity nor a history of cooperation, however, is apt to remain relevant when one puts on the uniform and the identity of an anonymous soldier. In the identity of soldier, one has to work very hard to be able to contemplate peace. Such anonymity, together with the anonymity of the others who may have been friends after the tsunami, but now are defined as enemies, does not allow for the human connection that would foster peace. In military uniforms, the call to aggression trumps the call to collaboration. Risks are not perceived as shared, but as distributed in accordance with one's strength and the power of one's weapons. The tasks are not shared; they are in opposition.

The resources are not shared; they are the basis of conflict. What the fisherman said fit modern principles of social psychology. The circumstances are very powerful. People sometimes act in ways that are quite atypical as a result of the situation they are in. On the sea, shared goals, shared identity as fisherman, and shared risks, all are situational cues that tell you to cooperate with all the rest of the ship's fishermen. In military uniform, exactly the opposite cues tell you to cooperate only with your side. The same is true, in nonviolent form, of course, in sports. Outside the arena, all lacrosse, football, or basketball players share a common bond and identity. Once the uniforms are on and the game begins, the identity is not as an athlete, but as a member of this one particular team, and it is a fight to the finish.

As the afternoon conversation continued, and we relaxed into what I understood then, and understand now, to be mutual understanding and respect, I recognized that the Fisherman, who described himself as "uneducated," had a depth of human understanding and perspective that was far beyond impressive—it reflected a grasp of the complexity and multiple interactions of ethnic conflict that very few people—educated or not—ever reach. He worried about the island, and the island's place in the world. He worried about his children and all the children on the island—not only those of his ethnicity or his religion, but all the children. Although he is one man of one ethnic group, he was able to see the sadness and pain caused by the conflict itself—by all sides, rather than by the other group alone. He was able to entertain a knowledgeable perspective on the needs of the island in the world at large, as well as the needs of various groups on the island.

In our entire conversation, the Fisherman never said that one group was right and the other wrong; one group good and the other bad; one group was virtuous and the other evil. He did not blame his own or any other group. Rather, he said he was sad for the problem of all groups not getting along, and all groups, as well as the island and the world, suffering as a result. Sad, ashamed, and concerned. He considered various options: people could stop fighting on their own, which did not seem likely; outside countries could intervene—also not likely. Perhaps only God could help. He discussed religion, but did not suggest that his own religion was best, right, or even better than any others. At first this may sound like the thoughts of a person who has a laissez faire, "live and let live" attitude—where the belief is that all religions are alike, and one is as good as another. But upon listening closely, it became clear that the Fisherman was saying something quite different. He was saying that he has a deep belief and convictions that spring from that. He is a dedicated and devout man. Reflecting on his own devout adherence and the comfort he receives from his faith, he realizes that others may well feel as he does, even if they feel that way about a different faith and set of beliefs. His respect for others comes not out of a failure of care, nor out of a failure of faith, but out of intensity of both faith and care. He does not propose that all religions are alike, but he realizes that others may feel as strongly about their religion as he

does about his own, whether they agree with one another or not. Undoubtedly, there are Israelis who feel the same about Palestinian Muslims, and Palestinian Muslims who feel the same about Israelis, but their voices are drowned out by the voices of those who are inclined to assign goodness and badness in the conflict. And so is the Fisherman's perspective drowned out.

Psychologists who study our ability to understand relationships and interactions tell us that this capacity to sincerely and consistently take such a view of the people engaged in a complex and multiparty conflict, and of the conflict in relation to the community and the global community, is only characteristic of about 5 percent of the world's population. Most of the rest of us fall into choosing sides, assigning blame, and justifying the actions of "our" side, or at best, looking only as far as the conflict itself, without reference to the larger global context of the conflict. Most of us believe that our group is usually only acting in self-defense and that the other group is usually the aggressor. Even if we did not like certain actions taken by our side, most of us would still think our side had been treated unfairly, and was the more virtuous side, on the whole. Many of us would not want even want to associate closely with members of the other group, whether in a shared project or in a shared neighborhood.

Even among scholars studying war and terrorism from a distance, very few can take and maintain a view as mature as that of the Fisherman. The capacity to do so when one is in the midst of the conflict itself is even more impressive than when one is an observer, and nearly impossible when one is in a community of people who are convinced that their side—which is also your "side"—is correct. Imagine how rare it is, for example, for an American to look at something like an Olympic competition and say that it is a wonderful experience to see all these hard-working athletes, and that it is not so important what country wins the most gold medals as it is that the countries can cooperate to hold the Olympic competition. Think about how unusual it would be for someone from your home area to say that it was not important what American baseball team won the World Series, or what actress won the Oscar. It is a great deal harder to take that kind of view in relation to ethnic conflict, in relation to a war where one's loved ones very lives are at stake. Some people can do that, but not many.

The Fisherman not only articulated this point of view, but he acted on it. In his community, he was one of a group of people appointed to help in the resolution of local conflicts, which often reflected, on a personal scale, the divisions that also existed island-wide. As a result of this and the shared fishing expedition, he actually knew the members of all sides to the ongoing conflict as persons, with strengths and weaknesses, virtues and flaws. He saw members of his own group as not totally unlike members of the other groups.

Perhaps an American counterpart would be someone who was a member of a neighborhood interfaith or interracial council called to assist a community in its efforts to come together after a series of symbolically hateful messages had

been scrawled in graffiti, across a building or a bridge. In such situations, those chosen must be able to see the real enemy as *the potential devastation of a community*, rather than see the enemy as the persons who are similar to, or supportive of, the victims, or the persons who are similar to, or supportive of, those who are suspected of creating the graffiti. This is harder than it sounds, for everyone on such a council is also closely related, in one way or another, to a party of the conflict. For example, if there are hateful phrases scrawled against American Muslim families in a neighborhood, the interfaith council called together must, of necessity, consist of Muslim and non-Muslim members. It must consist of neighbors and friends of Muslims and neighbors and friends of non-Muslims, and neighbors and friends of people who think the Muslims are posing a threat to the community. Even if they have some reservations about each other, and even if some of them still have feelings left over about 9/11, or about terrorism in Israel, and even if the Muslims have feelings about the way they have been profiled and misunderstood just because of their religion, the Jewish, Christian, Buddhist, Hindu, and Muslim members of the committee must work with one another, forming a bond or group that transcends their differences, and that transcends their connections to others in the community. They must be willing to disappoint some of their friends, neighbors, and family members, who may want them to rid the community of Muslims, or some friends, neighbors, or family members who the committee to refuse to hear the point of view of those who fear Muslims, in order to support the community as a whole. In order to do that, they must agree that the greatest threat is not from the Muslims and also not from the anti-Muslims, but from the intensity of the conflict, the possibility of hate dominating relationships in the community, and the potential disorder, destabilization, or even demise of the community itself.

Those engaged in the interfaith or interracial group may have friends and family who do not understand, and who even think they are being disloyal to their own group or religion by working closely with those who might be part of a group that is the enemy of the group to which they belong. The Jewish friend of a Jewish member of the interfaith council may find it puzzling to see his friend defending an American of Iranian heritage who is an active Shiite Muslim. The Christian friend of a Christian committee member may question whether their friend is making it easier for those from a "terrorist" country to settle in the community, and may worry that this friend is engaged in unwise action that might cause a threat to his children. But the members of the Interfaith Council must be more mature, wiser, and better able to maintain a balanced and deliberate view of the situation. They must be willing to be questioned by their friends and family. They must make it clear that they are not saying that all religions are alike or that the differences are unimportant, or that they do not care. What they must say is that everyone must be allowed to experience intense and devout adherence to the religion they choose, while the community remains safe, secure, and stable.

On a Global Scale: The Fisherman's Potential Network

Around the world, there are many individuals and small groups who success-fully transcend their own ethnic, national, or religious group's view, in order to bring a period of peace and progress to their part of the world. These are people who—recognizing that there are other views, that those views have validity to the people who hold them, and that continuing intergroup conflict is harmful to the next generation—can be found on every continent and in many commun-ities. There are the Quakers, in many parts of the world, who have a long-standing commitment to work for peace and nonviolence. The Quakers or "Friends" pub-lish a newspaper called *Peacework* highlighting activities of their group and other groups working toward peace.[2] There is also the Parents' Circle, a group of Israeli and Palestinian families who have lost a loved one to the war, and committed themselves to work with others from Palestine and Israel, toward peace, rather than revenge.[3] Sarvodaya is a highly respected and recognized international peace organization based in Sri Lanka.[4] There are many, many less well-known organi-zations dedicated to building peace. In various communities, there are Restorative Justice projects, where those who feel wronged meet the person whom, they feel, wronged them and talk together, and where revenge is replaced by restoration or substitution. There are projects around the world with a Truth and Justice model, where those who have experienced violations of human rights and those who are accused of violations of their rights meet to interrupt the ongoing patterns. The Public Conversations project in Watertown, Massachusetts encourages commun-ities to engage in discussions of many difficult topics, and helps with advice, con-sultation, and in-house discussion. The group has sponsored ongoing talks between those who have seen themselves as adversaries, including those who refer to themselves as pro-life and those who refer to themselves as pro-choice.[5] In Ann Arbor, Michigan, six Jewish-American and six Arab-American women have been meeting twice a month for several years in order to get to know each other and understand each other's points of view. Their work is documented in the film *Refusing to be Enemies.* They now assist similar groups, as well. Information about the group and the film are on their Web site.[6] In the United States, a group of family therapists (American Family Therapy Association, or AFTA) who had lived in, or had strong connections with, areas of war, have written eloquently about the difficulty, as well as the necessity, of understanding the perspectives of others (Jodie Kliman 2005). Large and small international grassroots and non-governmental agencies also work toward mutual understanding, as an alternative to never-ending revenge.

Arguably the most powerful little known of these groups is Pugwash, an international group of distinguished scientists who won the Nobel Prize for their work in preventing nuclear war. They meet without great fanfare or media atten-tion, and work across differences in ethnicity, religion, and race, but with a

shared belief in the importance of science as a tool for the common good, rather than mutual annihilation. They have considerable international influence because of the standing of their members, and the connections of their members. The members are not naïve or simplistic in any way. They know the limited role they can play. They also know how to have fun. But they are aware of the serious nature of their shared mission: no less than to save human civilization from destruction resulting from human foibles.[7]

This is just a small sample of many groups that include noteworthy people and include ordinary people who have decided to get away from mutual blame, and move toward mutual collaboration—not always because of religion, or because of belief in the morality of such a stance, but because they feel there is no other viable choice, if the human race is to survive, than to attempt to understand the point of view of the "other" and respect it. We are beginning to assemble a list of such small and large groups, and will post it on our Web site.[8]

Many in the world have not been aware of these groups, and have not been aware of their own capacity to transcend differences. Most individuals, groups, and networks do not yet think this way because most have never considered this option, and have never met anyone who truly thinks this way. And some who know this way of thinking exists do not like it, and even discourage it, because if many people thought this way, it would strip them of the power gained by inciting their followers to fear and hate the "other" and convincing the followers that, in order to be safe, they must continue to follow them. These leaders offer false promises of a rosy future that will come after the enemies are vanquished or killed, when vanquishing and killing leads only to the false illusion of a rosy future. Indeed, in encouraging loyalty to the in-group, they wittingly or unwittingly encourage hatred, violence, and fear of the other group. Besides government leaders encouraging war, there are many individuals and groups who benefit financially from war, and who—wittingly or unwittingly—do their part to encourage the continuation of war, conflict, and terrorism. Social scientist Marc Pilisuk has described in some detail how this works, and who, in fact, does benefit from war (Pilisuk and Rountree, 2008). In stark contrast with the Fisherman and with his visible and invisible network are those who either cannot or will not focus on the overall conflict, on the good of the community, or even on the survival of civilization, but instead focus on divisions, blame others, and do not look to eventual collaborations.

Good Guys and Bad Guys: "The Bad Guys Keep on Coming"[9]

To some readers, the phrase "bad guys" may bring to mind images of children playing make believe games. American children have been playing "Good guys and bad guys" for generations. Teacher/author Vivian Paley described some attributes of imaginary bad guys in her book called, *Bad Guys Don't Have*

Birthdays: Fantasy Play at Four (1988). Here are a few examples she provided from her students: "Bad guys don't have names so they can't have birthdays" (p. 5). "Bad guys can't have ladders," an explanation given by a young child for a story in which a bad guy gets stuck in a well, when a *good guy* had, moments earlier, climbed out of the same well on a ladder (p. 87), and "Bad guys have to steal from other bad guys," an explanation for the child's theory that good guys don't have things stolen from them (p. 31). We can see from these quotes that, for these young children, the phrase "bad guys" has a connotation: they are disadvantaged, and they will eventually, inevitably, be defeated. They may be bad, but they are surely not invincible.

Older children, play good and evil in more specific terms. Children get their ideas for identities of *bad guys* from the media, and we casually assume that these assignments are harmless. But we make that assumption at our own risk. When children use terms like *bad guy* when describing real people (even though they do not know such people)—Native Americans, Russians, Japanese, Arabs—they are teaching each other and themselves to support those media stereotypes. They are confident in assigning badness to all members of a group. And we, as adults, often come perilously to doing the same. For members of one of those stereotyped groups, it hits hard to realize that even at young ages, children of another group are socializing one another to see them as bad guys. When children played "Cowboys and Indians," without a thought for who real Indians are, or when they assigned badness to Russian, Japanese, or Arabs, without knowing anyone of that group, any child of the current media-fed stereotype who may have been, or may be, among them, of course, knows very well who some real live members of the stereotyped group are, and is likely to be puzzled and distressed at the stereotypes being played out.

It is, of course, entirely possible and even likely that the children who are assigning a modern ugly stereotype to an actual group are unaware of the impact on the real classmate of that group, and also unaware of the impact on themselves. An imaginary, unnamed, unidentified bad guy is one thing. But what about a bad guy who is identified with an ethnic group when a member of that ethnic group is in the room? Child's play that separates the world into bad guys and good guys reflects a low level of cognitive complexity—perhaps all that we can expect of children.

But the phrase "*The bad guys just keep coming,*" that begins this section does not come from child's play. It comes from *The Economist,* a highly respected publication with an upscale readership in the EU and the United States. It was the title of a recent (May 2007) article about increasing numbers—what appears to be an endless supply—of terrorists in the Middle East.[10] And the editors did not even see a need to put the term *bad guys* in quotes. The *International Herald Tribune* has also used the phrase to describe wrongdoers, including terrorists. The prestigious Council on Foreign Relations has a link, on its Web site, to a

paper published in the *Tribune,* called, *The Bad Guys Know What They're Doing,* referring to the knowledge and skill that was displayed in the poisoning of Alexander Litvenenko.[11] CNN reported that President George W. Bush, in 2002, used the term *bad guy* to describe Jose Padilla, and justify his detention.[12] And in 2008, Assistant Secretary of State Richard Boucher used the term in an interview with public radio. When it was suggested that negotiation might be useful in Pakistan after the assassination of Benazir Bhutto, Boucher responded,

> You could try it, but I think we've always found that a negotiation that's not backed by a certain amount of force can't really force out the bad guys who are up there and need to be taken care of.

On the one hand, the term "bad guys" is descriptive and may seem rather harmless. Perhaps, like children on the schoolyard, adults using the term mean to indicate that for terrorists, as for the imaginary "bad guys" in child's play, it is only a matter of time—they are doomed to fail and be defeated. On the other hand, it is surprising, and even a bit disturbing, to hear such a global, nonspecific, and even vague term used by grown men and women in positions of power and influence to describe people believed to be adversaries. At the very least would seem wise to be able to describe adversaries and why they are adversaries in a bit more detail. It is jarring to hear the suggestion that all we need to know about a person is that the person is "bad." It may well be that Padilla posed a threat; clearly he was judged to pose a threat. It would be hard for most Americans to judge how much threat and whether it was justified to detain him, if all the information available was that he is seen as a *bad guy.* Indeed the very concept of a person being *bad* makes no contribution to the nearly universally hoped for, eventual process of peace-seeking, that the Fisherman's comments suggest is so urgently needed.

We generally do not expect children at play to be able to explain what is bad about their bad guy in specific terms, for their world is simple and categorical, the "bad guy" is imaginary. The one-dimensional bad guy reflects childlike thought patterns, where categories are rigidly and simply defined, reflecting limitations in the ability to manage complex ideas, or complexity in people, who tend not to be all good or all bad. Besides, in the world of young children, fantasy and reality can be mixed. But while we do not expect four-year-olds to be specific or accountable for their global accusations of a figure as "bad"—it would seem we have a right to expect it of professionals, world leaders, and the press.

While use of the term *bad guy* makes the person so designated seem doomed, it makes the speaker sound as if they are less clear in their analysis than might be desirable. One disturbing thing about the use of the term "bad guys" by adult leaders to describe their adversaries is that it seems to indicate that those who should have known the most about those adversaries know very little, or think that very little is worth knowing. Describing such an enemy with just the word

bad suggests that our enemies are one-dimensional and indistinguishable. More importantly, it will make it much harder in the future, for us to collaborate with them, and seek to make peace with them. Terms like "bad guy," coming from leaders and the press, can incite a great increase in fear and hatred of the adversary. A brief look at recent history should disavow anyone of the idea that terrorism will be won by a decisive victory, such as surrender. Who would surrender? Who would be victorious? Furthermore, even those who surrender and those to whom they surrender must ultimately work together toward lasting peace. Those who were adversaries at one time were collaborators at another time. To continue to use the term, and concept, that terrorists are *bad guys* would be to suggest that all our adversaries could be lumped together, in one indiscriminate mob: *bad guys,* which could then be compared with everyone else, who must be, presumably, *good guys,* if only by contrast. It suggests that vanquishing them or "taking care of them" as Boucher said, or rendering them unable to harm us is our only task. But that, it turns out, is not at all likely to be true in the twenty-first century, and surely not with terrorism.

If the people who have been called *bad guys* were one-dimensional, like those in Ms. Paley's class, perhaps the *good guys* could win a war on terror by just getting rid of, or detaining, all those who were bad guys so that only good guys would remain free agents. When we see the devastation wrought by terrorists in New York, in Israel, in Madrid, in London, and in Tokyo, it is hard to think that they are anything other than *bad guys.* Hard as it is to believe, and incredible as it seems to those well-intentioned Americans who only want to live their lives safely, those same people that American leaders and press call *bad guys* have family, friends, and supporters who see them as *good guys,* and who see American leaders as *bad guys,* and they are every bit as convinced of their views on Americans and Europeans, as Americans and Europeans are convinced of their own fundamental goodness. Hard as it is to believe after hearing the rhetoric of *bad guys,* experienced diplomats around the world do not see us winning a war on terrorism using guns and bombs.

Managing the Difficult View

And, despite the despicable acts of terrorists, if we do not wish to advance the never-ending cycle of revenge, we must, like the Fisherman, and like the Americans on the interfaith or interracial councils, extend our vision beyond the specific actions of terrorists, and beyond the specific actions of counterterrorists seeking revenge, in order to consider the well-being of communities, large and small, including the global community. We must consider the possibility that the real enemy is not the terrorist or the antiterrorist, not the so-called *bad guys,* but the possibility that ongoing war and terrorism will lead to the destabilization, or even the end, of civilization itself. Marie Jones, in her plan *Night in*

November, describes a moment of such enlightenment on the part of Kenny, an Ulsterman who, watching a football match in Belfast becomes reviled by both sides' hatred and ashamed of his own people. He looks around him and says, "...surely to Christ these are not the people I am part of...no, it's not, don't tell me, I'm not hearing them..." (Jones Marie 2000, p. 73). Kenny is perhaps the Everyman who any of us could become. "This is not a football match," he says, recognizing the hatred on both sides. "It's a battlefield" (p. 73).

In the book called *The Oath,* author Khassan Baiev (2004) provides a lengthy stunning example of a community caring for young soldiers who are part of the group perceived as "the enemy." It was unthinkable to the community not to shelter and hide these soldiers, no matter what harm they might have done. The host family was able to call on an informal network to communicate with the soldiers' mothers, who then came to get them. The mothers, astonished by the kindness of the community they had perceived as enemies, pledge to bring their new-found truth, their experience of kindness from the community, to their loved ones and friends. But the author does not make much of this. Perhaps he understands that in a struggle such as theirs, one incident of kindness will not be enough.

Hearts and Minds?

In order to begin to "win" the "war on terrorism," according to most American and international experts on matters of state (Foreign Policy, 2006) we must think of it as a war for hearts and minds, rather than a war of guns and bombs. But very few of us can even imagine a war for hearts and minds. How would we win the hearts and minds of terrorists, or of the supporters of terrorism? Some would wonder—do they even have hearts? And in spite of the passionate feelings of victimization and of having been wronged, and in spite of knowing that family members and friends are at risk of dying in another terrorist attack, we must reach beyond our usual approach, beyond our focus on the deadly acts they may be capable of, and recognize that somewhere on this small globe, someone—many people, in fact—are wondering the very same thing about us.

Indeed, while youth in the United States know very little about the countries where child soldiers are common, many of the youth in those countries learn a great deal about the United States, including how it spends its money, how much of the world's resources it uses, and which governments it supports. They know where their own government gets its resources, including weapons and money. They know that every country's resources are finite. They know that the United States and the EU make choices. And they agree with Dwight D. Eisenhower, who said, in the Chance For Peace Address Washington, DC, April 16, 1953,

> Every gun made, every warship launched, every rocket fired signifies, in the final sense, a theft from those who hunger and are not fed, those who are

cold and are not clothed....This is not a way of life at all....Under the cloud of threatening war, it is humanity hanging from a cross of iron.

Youth tend to make judgments on simple matters such as where the money goes. If we want to win their hearts and minds, we had better not be hypocritical. We had better have our own priorities where we believe theirs should be.

The Rest of the Story

Noted clinical psychologist Dr. Donald Meichenbaum, one of the developers of the most effective type of psychotherapy available at this time, when interviewing clients, seeks not only to hear about their pathology, but, he emphasizes, he wants to hear "the rest of the story." He wants to know their strengths, their resiliency, their passions, their capacity for good and healthy behavior. In short, he is committed to understanding the whole person of the patient, not only the patient's pathology. When we are thinking about children who become terrorists, who engage in violent actions, who even plan to die in a violent action, we also need to know the "rest of the story." We cannot stop at the fact that they are willing to kill others, horrifying as that is to contemplate. We have to listen hard to find out what they have been through and why they have come to this point. We have to understand that they have families and loved ones, and are thinking of their act as pro-social. Like Carmen and the young terrorists in Ann Patchett's novel, they want to "Free the people." Like Updike's young Ahmad, they want to do what they understand will please their God. They want to influence people toward what they think is a better way of being. And they are willing to die for those purposes, purposes that most Americans will think are misguided. However, guiding them in better paths will not ever come about through war.

Many psychology students—past and present—remember Maslow's hierarchy, or pyramid, of needs. That pyramid makes intuitive sense to mainstream American students. The pyramid suggests that it is difficult, if not impossible, to think about care and love for or from others—even those close to us—if we do not have an adequate supply of air, or if we are hungry, thirsty, or do not have shelter from the elements. Furthermore, it suggests that we cannot think about education, or embrace morality, or shed prejudice if we have not met our basic needs; that is, if we are in a state of deficiency. This pyramid suggests that children whose parents, despite their best efforts, cannot protect them from repeated hunger, repeated assault, and lack of safety—who cannot even provide clean water or air—cannot be expected to become loving and caring educated individuals who seek fulfillment in education or the arts, who are free of prejudice, or who accept conventional standards of morality. (There are, of course, notable exceptions to this.) From this pyramid, you might predict that those who are starving may be at risk of acting in immoral or even violent ways for the sake

of survival. However, you would not predict that they would understand or care about a political or religious cause, or be likely to consider the cause important enough, to engage in it, while starving. You would certainly not predict that they would be able to mobilize in well-organized groups to perpetrate violence, war, or terrorism.

You might, however, consider the possibility that children who are poor and hungry, and whose families cannot protect them, might respond to being fed, clothed, housed, and promised protection by an apparently strong individual or group. They might become loyal to that individual or group who saved them from misery. That might be true whether the group was a group that taught nonviolence or a group that taught violence. And you might further predict that poor and unprotected children would be weak enough, and their families would be weak enough, that they could be bullied and threatened into joining paramilitary or terrorist organizations. Thus Maslow's hierarchy, while it does not predict who will start of be passionate about a political movement based on poverty, does predict who might be recruited or coerced—two major ways that children end up as soldiers and as terrorists.

How is it that a paramilitary that is in hiding and not part of mainstream society would have the resources, supplies, etc. to mount a military-style campaign, and also entice poor children to join the campaign? How can they compete with such international organizations with public support as UNICEF, the Red Cross or Red Crescent, or Save the Children? It might be useful here to describe the likely flow of resources that account for the paramilitaries' ability to recruit.

In very rough, outline form, here is what appears to happen. Money is secretly funneled to the organization by people who support its ends. They may be local people with a small amount of resources to share. They may also be expatriates who send funds back to the home country. In most cases, these funds go solely to support the families of the expatriate. However, some of these funds, directly or indirectly, reach the paramilitary groups. The groups then use these funds to buy the resources needed to provide adequately for their troops—including basic needs and training needs. With the funds to feed, clothe, house, and train its recruits, the group expands. Some of the expansion includes children who will later become engaged in terrorist acts. The children, loyal to their leader, or forced to obey the leader under threat, participate in such actions, believing, perhaps, that they are leading ultimately, to good things for their own families, or at least to revenge on the soldiers whom they have believe have harmed their loved ones, and on those in power whom they believe have violated the human rights of their loved ones. Ultimately, the children are led to believe that they are doing pro-social acts, or else they are led to believe that if they do not do as they are told, they and their families will be tortured, raped, or killed.

This is not the sequence followed in Palestine, but it is the sequence followed in many areas of the world where there are terrorists. In Palestine, as noted earlier,

there is likely to be money funneled from external sources, but recruits are chosen because of their devoutness and ordinariness, and are told that they are doing the will of Allah, and that they, their friends, and their families, will be rewarded. They are altruistic, and they are being used by desperate, possibly ruthless, possibly even cowardly, adults who do not mind seeing children die for the political and social gains their organization desires. These adults, and other adults in other parts of the world, who send children to their deaths, may ultimately be the hardest of the terrorists to imagine collaborating with. It takes a big stretch of imagination to consider the possibility.

Child Terrorists Who Are Immigrants in the EU and the United States

Children and young adults who are outside the country, but who identify with the oppressed group, or perhaps with all oppressed groups, will be inclined to join in what they see as actions toward liberation of the people. Their efforts may be guided toward working within the system, or toward working outside the system; toward bringing about peace, or toward strengthening the paramilitary, or terrorist, organizations. For example, various students from local Boston area colleges, having learned about the plight of children in a war-torn country, having understood that the real enemy in the country was the ongoing war without resolution, took that into account in deciding what to do. Some of them are bringing aid, and others using videorecorders in a country with ethnic conflict, in order to bring the situation of all children of that country to awareness for a larger audience, who, they hope, will put pressure on international bodies to work toward peace.

Some other young adults, who identify with all oppressed people, might have taken a different path. Perhaps if they had become convinced that the oppressed people were in the right—were *good guys*—and that the oppressors were *bad guys*—they might have decided to use clandestine means to funnel money or supplies to the paramilitary forces. Or if they had become convinced that the oppressed people were *bad guys,* they might have worked to bring about greater support for the government of the country, lobbying international bodies to send arms and funds to the government to aid in its attempts to eradicate the paramilitary organization.

Winning Hearts and Minds: A Modest Proposal

For adults who engage in terrorism, social science research suggests that the most likely and strongest motivations are probably not poverty or lack of educational opportunity. Child terrorists, however, as we have seen, are more like child soldiers than like adult terrorists. They may be more easily recruited or coerced if they are poor, hungry, and lacking opportunity for education. Nevertheless, child

and adult terrorists may have some motivations in common. Alan Krueger and Jitka Maleckova conclude that what they call "political conditions" including lack of civil rights, as well as "longstanding feelings of indignity and frustration" are more likely to predict involvement with terrorism than are poverty or lack of education (p. 119). This is what the social scientists at the conference described in chapter 2 of this book called "grievances." These conditions are similar to the conditions that Kenneth Hardy and Tracey Laszloffy describe as conditions fostering violence in teenagers in the United States. In their book *Teens Who Hurt,* they describe adolescents who would rather risk death than be disrespected, with the phrase "death before dis" (p. 43). It is useful to recognize that in some cultures indignity is worse than poverty, and worse than death itself, possibly contributing to the acceptance of planned death in a terrorist attack. It is also useful to realize that the degree of indignity suffered by Arabs in and out of the Middle East is extreme, and that the Arab culture is one of those where indignity, or lack of respect, is intolerable. David Shipler's book (2002), *Arab and Jew: Wounded Spirits in the Promised Land,* details some of the indignities suffered by Arabs in the Middle East. And author Pradeep Jeganathan, in some short stories called *At the Water's Edge,* provides insight into the kind of indignity suffered by ethnic Tamil youth in Sri Lanka. He describes a young Tamil boy, a student in what we might call a prep school, evidently the only Tamil in his class. Another student says to him, "This is our land, the Sinhala Land, and we have to clean out scum like you. Prince Duttu-Gamunu did it before..." referring to a medieval battle depicted on a mural on the classroom wall (Pradeep Jaganathan 2004, p. 9) Psychologists have found that verbal indignities, when tolerated or ignored, may lead to more violent hate crimes.

Before leaving the topic of indignities and human rights, let us consider the effects on children when their parents lack civil rights or lack human rights. In Sri Lanka, for example, human rights violations include kidnapping and disappearances, which the well-regarded organization Human Rights Watch documents clearly is attributable to the government. Children know about kidnappings and disappearances. Many have friends or relatives who have disappeared. As I was told before I went to Sri Lanka, the government has a habit of causing the disappearance of teenagers just before they are likely to be recruited by the Tamil Tigers.

So while I do not think we can win the hearts and minds of those whom we do not help when they are desperate for help with the basic elements for survival, whose pain and losses we do not acknowledge, while we continue to consume such a disproportionate share of the earth's resources, I also do not think we can win the hearts and minds of those who suffer continuing indignity, lack of equal rights, unacknowledged losses, and stereotyping by the international community unless we participate in efforts to stop these violations, and make our stance clear and public.

While we do not think the United States should be the world's police officer, we do think the United States could easily become a role model and the world's most vocal champion of human rights, both as a state and as part of international organizations such as the United Nations. If we want civilization to survive, we cannot allow our government to be timid about speaking out to countries that violate human rights because those governments take a public antiterrorism stance. The government cannot change course easily, unless the citizens demand it.

We believe the United States has an obligation to de-escalate global panic about terrorism, and to try to help stabilize global society by assisting in efforts toward mutual negotiation—to do on a global scale what the Fisherman does in his village: To take a long view of conflict and violence, and to see the true enemy not as terrorists or antiterrorists, but as the risk of deterioration into endless revenge, destabilization of communities and societies, and perhaps of civilization itself.

Perhaps more important, citizens could demand that our government begin to work toward peace through the exercise of compassion, care, and generosity toward those who are in grave need as a core element of its foreign policy. That would be to advertise and expand on the American spirit of generosity—a spirit that many of the world's people do not understand. If the government cannot yet give up its reputation as the world's toughest tough guy, it could perhaps add to that reputation, the image of a compassionate and sophisticated tough guy, a tough guy as advanced as the Fisherman.

American Compassion and Mercy

In fact, the U.S. military does perform many acts of mercy and compassion—acts that no one but the military could do—rescue missions and transport missions of mercy that require sophisticated technology that only the military can provide. However, the scope of these actions is not often known to civilians, either here or in other parts of the world. Drawing national and international attention to the ways in which our military is involved in complex rescue operations and in mercy acts such as transporting sick children to care facilities, for example, would be helpful in winning hearts and minds. But much of this is drowned out by awareness of the U.S. citizens' record on greedy use of the world's resources, and by our government taking sides in disputes where we might have had an opportunity to be more helpful as peacemaker, and our condoning of violence in many parts of the world. When we asked the children we talked to in Sri Lanka how the other countries could help end the war there, some of them said very directly and clearly that the United States could help if it would stop providing weapons to the government, and if they would encourage both sides to end the war. Fortunately, several months later the United States

has withdrawn its military aid, due to the evidence of human rights abuses by the government, and made restoration of that aid contingent on the government demonstrating to the United States that it has met basic criteria. This sort of decision is to be applauded and will do a lot to win hearts and minds.

Knowing Hearts and Minds

We can hardly win hearts and minds of people we do not know, or whom we take to be one-dimensionally *bad*. The "bad guys" in Ms. Paley's class are indeed imaginary figures of a single dimension: badness. But *The Economist, the International Herald Tribune,* Assistant Secretary of State Boucher and President Bush were talking about real, identifiable, complex people, and, hard as it may be to believe at times, they have families and communities that love, respect, and support them, even after their deaths. In their own minds, and the minds of their families and supporters—misguided as those minds might be, in many cases neither the terrorists nor their communities see what they do as bad, but rather they see it as good, and even altruistic. They see their deaths as potentially bringing the world's attention to an impossible situation, and they do not see them as *bad guys*. If we do not get to know them, by, as playwright Robin Soans suggests, talking to them, we will surely not be able to win their hearts and minds.

Why Try to Understand Those Who Would Perpetrate Violence on Innocent People?

Many Americans who have an image of the burning twin towers engraved in their minds, hearts, and souls, may very well only be able to see the 9/11 terrorists as *bad guys*. From the point of view of some of those who lost loved ones, not much else about the terrorists matters except for the terrible acts that turned the lives of so many good and decent Americans upside down. Perhaps those most affected should not be expected to participate in a conversation about winning the hearts and minds of the rest of the world's potential terrorists and of the communities that support them. But for those who wish to and can, the effort to understand the terrorists, from the terrorists' own point of view, as reflected in the works of authors like Soans, Moghaddam, Gerges, Jones, Updike, Patchett, and others, will be rewarded. At the very least, those with the courage to try will have a better understanding of the twenty-first-century world. And those who try, even when it is painful and difficult, to understand those who support terrorists, will be in the company of brave and intelligent historical and contemporary figures who also tried, for the sake of their children and all future generations of children. Like the citizens on interracial or interfaith councils, but on a larger scale, these are people who try to see the problem as not the terrorists and not

the antiterrorists, but the never-ending violence between terrorists and antiterrorists that threatens to destabilize and even destroy civilization as we know it. These are people who favor diplomacy and negotiation, as a means toward a global civilization that can survive.

Northern Ireland

A very instructive, contemporary model of diplomacy leading to a complex, multitiered solution to an ongoing ethnic and religious conflict is the resolution of the situation in Northern Ireland. After years of hatred and violence, even those who hated each other began to see that a negotiated diplomatic multiparty solution was desirable. They were not immediately hailed by their parties as heroes. In a chronology posted on PBS Frontline Web site, there is a note from October 13, 1997, saying

> British Prime Minister Tony Blair meets with a Sinn Fein delegation and shakes hands with Martin McGuinness and Gerry Adams in East Belfast. Northern Ireland's Protestant majority are outraged, citing the IRA's history of violence and continued unwillingness to lay down their weapons.[13]

But they shouldered on, for a very long time, and in the end a settlement was reached. Ten years later, it is holding with an ongoing and evidently rather vigorous monitoring process. The United States did assist with this negotiated settlement, and former Senator George Mitchell is widely credited as having had an essential role in the creation of the "Good Friday Agreement" reached in Belfast in 1998. The agreement was reached by ongoing negotiations that included terrorist organizations and antiterrorist organizations, and the agreement included early release of some who had been detained for terrorist acts. It may be surprising to realize that, in recent history, various negotiated cease-fires and agreements have included parties accused of terrorism, just as negotiated peace treaties often include parties who had caused harm to one another. Beginning shortly after September 11, 2001, however, the press and government officials have stated that we would not negotiate with terrorists. Such a decision would seem to be at odds with documented breakthroughs in ongoing conflict, all of which have required parties who condemned each other to find the courage to sit down together to create peace. This is not done out of an ideal of love for all or out of an ideal of turning the other cheek. It is not done with blindness to the capacity of the parties for violence, for subterfuge, and for sabotage. The brave parties to such talks must be protected from their own enthusiastic group members who see them as traitors. It is done, rather, because it is the only path out of never-ending revenge and violence, the only way for our children and all children to have a chance to be productive and to grow up with hope for a future with opportunity, or for any future at all.

Challenging Misperceptions: Everyday Heroism

A young veteran of the Iraq war told me that he had a gun pointed on a child and was prepared to shoot, thinking the child might pose a threat. This was an extremely painful situation for the young man, a father himself, for he did not want to shoot, and yet he knew that children were sometimes used as weapons, and this child was coming toward him, carrying something that looked suspicious. The child, aware or not, might have been a threat to his life. Indeed, his superior gave him the order to shoot, but he broke orders by waiting a moment, hoping he would find out that the child was innocent. In that moment, he found out that the "weapon" the child was carrying was actually a broken cell phone he had found. For a moment, to that soldier's superior, the child was nothing more than a "bad guy," a threat. But it had been a misperception. The young veteran had saved the child from an untimely death. He had done so as a father, not only to his own children, but in identification with all fathers and all sons. But he had done more. He had contributed to a better view of American soldiers, a small step in the direction of winning hearts and minds.

Not all of us have experiences as part of our everyday life that can lead to the kind of heroism that the young veteran had shown. But there are things that all of us can do to be a bit more like the veteran and more like the Fisherman, if we can make our own the idea that the real enemy is endless war, and the real way to win is by winning hearts and minds. Everyone chooses his own path. We would never have predicted that college students would take the lesson that war is the enemy and go to document its effects, nor would we have suggested they do so. We are social scientists and we do what social scientists do: think, write, and teach others. Others may be activists whose skills and inclinations lead them to organize others to lobby congressmen and congresswomen to keep pressuring countries with human rights violations to change. Some may join those efforts, or simply write to congress and the White House.

Others may simply say a few words, ask a few questions, when they hear their members of their family or friends talking about "bad guys." Some may join the Peace Corps, or just go on an international trip as a volunteer to help, using their skills as teachers, medical workers, engineers, mental health clinicians, carpenters, farmers, and the like, to bring about small changes that truly affect the quality of life in places where such changes are badly needed. Some may research the policies on detention, interrogation, and possible torture that the United States has engaged in recently, and ask their elected officials to consider the impact that word of these actions is making on the battle for hearts and minds.

The most important thing, though, that anyone can do, is probably to look within, to find the deep-seated tendency to split the world into good guys and bad guys, and to stretch beyond that comfortable zone of demarcation to see that such a split does not lead anywhere other than to endless hatred and endless

revenge. To consider walking a mile in the well-worn boots of a child who has seen tragedy firsthand, seen government soldiers raping or killing, been displaced, lost loved ones, had friends disappear, lived in a refugee camp, and then been taught that it is worthwhile, pro-social, and even altruistic to die in a violent act, who thinks that doing so will help to "Free the people."

Notes

Chapter 1

1. A recent Human Rights Watch report places the responsibility for most disappearances on the Sri Lankan government. The report says, "In the great majority of cases documented by Human Rights Watch and Sri Lankan groups, evidence indicates the involvement of government security forces—army, navy, or police. The Sri Lankan military, empowered by the country's counterterrorism laws, has long relied on extrajudicial means, such as "disappearances" and summary executions—in its operations against Tamil militants and JVP insurgents," http://hrw.org/reports/2008/srilanka0308/1.htm#_Toc191887309.

Chapter 2

1. Conference program online at www.societyforterrorismresearch.org.
2. Interview with Brian Jenkins, University of California, Irvine, 1988. Retrieved from http://www.lib.uci.edu/quest/index.php?page=jenkins.
3. See Wessells (2006a).
4. Retrieved on December 20, 2007, from http://www.nytimes.com/2007/12/15/business/15rich.html.
5. David Adams, one of the signers of the Seville Statement, has detailed the history of the statement, on a web page he maintains, called "Global Movement for a Culture of Peace" at http://www.culture-of-peace.info/ssov-intro.html. This statement, adopted by UNESCO, can be found on the Internet, at http://portal.unesco.org/education/en/ev.php-URL_ID=3247&URL_DO=DO_TOPIC&URL_SECTION=201.html.

Chapter 3

1. *LATimes,* January 20, 2008, retrieved from http://www.latimes.com/news/ nationworld/world/la-fg- arrests20jan20,1,6820770,print.story?coll=la-headlines-world&ctrack=1&cset=true.

2. For a good start at understanding the differences between collectivist societies and individualist societies, we suggest the book *Individualism and Collectivism,* by Triandis (2001).

Chapter 4

1. The *Sri Lanka Daily News* reported on December 31, 2007, "Forces' Chiefs predict Tiger Extinction in 2008." The article referred to commanders of the army, navy, and air force, http://www.dailynews.lk/2007/12/31/sec01.asp (accessed June 1, 2008).

Chapter 5

1. We found this quote attributed to Hoover on multiple Web sites. We were not able to verify that he actually said it, but it is consistent with his philosophy and world view as we understand it.

2. The well-respected British medical journal *Lancet* published, in October, 2006, a public health research study that led to an estimate of the number of civilian deaths attributable to the Iraq War—that is, deaths in excess of those that would have been expected had the death rate remained the same as it was before the war. Study authors from Johns Hopkins School of Public Health and from the School of Medicine at Al Mustansiriya University in Iraq, using well-regarded methodology, estimated the number of civilian deaths attributable to the war at 654,965.

3. We found this on multiple Web sites, including http://thinkexist.com/ quotes/jose_narosky/.

4. "Gold Star" mothers are those whose son or daughter has been killed in a war.

5. http://www.youtube.com/watch?v=fJuNgBkloFE (retrieved on March 21, 2008) CNNN—spoofs on American ignorance of world geography, events.

6. http://www.cnnnn.com/.

7. In 2001, PBS created programming for a "global classroom," called *Wide Angle.* Many programs are accessible online, along with educational supplementary material and guides. See http://www.pbs.org/wnet/wideangle/index.html.

8. http://www.snitt.no/mdtt/prints/movie.htm.

9. http://www.uis.unesco.org/en/stats/statistics/ed/map_illit_monde2000.jpg.

10. http://www.snitt.no/mdtt/prints/movie.htm.

11. Reporters Without Borders 2008 annual Report on Sri Lanka, http://www.rsf.org/article.php3?id_article=25690, retrieved on March 24, 2008.

12. According to the *International Herald Tribune,* December 18, 2007, the conditions for resuming aid are as follows: Secretary of State Rice must verify that the Sri Lankan government has done the following:

- prosecuted military officials alleged to have recruited child soldiers and committed extrajudicial executions.
- provided humanitarian groups and reporters access to Tamil areas of the country.
- agreed to allow the United Nations to establish a human rights office in the country. http://www.iht.com/articles/2007/12/18/asia/military.php.

13. The costs and risks associated with counterterrorism efforts have been carefully documented by Paul R. Kimmel and Chris E. Stout, *Collateral Damage,* ed. Chris E. Stout (Westport, CT: Praeger Press, 2006).

14. Ibid.

15. http://www.wand.org/.

16. http://www.pugwash.org/publication/op/feb2006.pdf .

17. Ibid.

Chapter 6

1. In this section, all phrases in quotation marks are the translated phrases. The words are the words of the translator, who attempted to make them closely reflect the words of the Fisherman.

2. http://www.peaceworkmagazine.org.

3. http://www.parentscircle.israel.net/.

4. http://www.sarvodaya.org.

5. http://www.publicconversations.org.

6. www.zeitouna.org.

7. http://www.pugwash.org.

8. www.creatingyoungmartyrs.com.

9. In this section, all phrases in quotation marks are the translated phrases. The words are the words of the translator, who attempted to make them closely reflect the words of the Fisherman.

10. http://www.economist.com/world/africa/displaystory.cfm?story_id=9122645.

11. http://www.cfr.org/bios/10786/?groupby=1&hide=1&id=10786&page=1.

12. http://www.cnn.com/2002/US/06/11/dirty.bomb.suspect/.

13. http://www.pbs.org/wgbh/pages/frontline/shows/ira/etc/cron.html.

References

Ahadi, Ali Samadi, and Oliver Stoltz. *Lost Children*. Germany: Joint Venture Video, 2005.

Allison, Graham. *Nuclear Terrorism: The Ultimate Preventable Catastrophe*. New York: Times Books, 2004.

Arnestad, Beate, and Morton Daae. *My Daughter the Terrorist*. Norway: Snitt Film Production, 2007.

Atran, Scott. "Genesis of Suicide Terrorism." *Science* 299, no. 5612, 1534–39, 2003.

Baiev, Khassan. *The Oath: A Surgeon Under Fire*. New York: Walker and Company, 2004.

Baird, Abigail, A., Bowser, Betty Ann, Giedd, Jay, Wellek, Mark, and Viner, Jane, Contributors to *The Teen Brain*. http://www.pbs.org/newshour/bb/science/july-dec04/brain_10-13.html (accessed on March 31, 2008).

Beah, Ismael. *A Long Way Gone: Memoirs of a Boy Soldier*. New York: Farrar, Straus, and Giroux, 2007.

Boutwell, Jeffrey, ed. *Addressing the Nuclear Weapons Threat: The Russell-Einstein Manifesto Fifty Years On*. Pugwash Conferences on Science and World Affairs, December 2005, 4, 1.

Briggs, Jimmie. *Innocents Lost: When Child Soldiers Go to War*. New York: Basic Books, 2005.

Bronfenbrenner, Urie. *Making Human Beings Human*. Thousand Oaks, CA: Sage, 2005.

Burnham, Gilbert, Riyadh Lafta, Shannon Doocy, and Les Roberts. "Mortality After the 2003 Invasion of Iraq: A Cross-sectional Cluster Sample Survey." *Lancet* 368 (2004): 1421–28.

Canada, Geoffrey. *Fist, Stick, Knife, Gun.* Boston: Beacon Press, 1995.

Commons, Michael Lamport, Edward James Trudeau, and Sharon Anne Stein. "Hierarchical Complexity of Tasks Shows the Existence of Developmental Stages." *Developmental Review* 18, no. 237, 278 (1998).

Erikson, Erik. *Childhood and Society.* New York: W.W. Norton and Co., 1954.

Erikson, Erik, Joan M. Erikson, and Helen Q. Kivnick. *Vital Involvement in Old Age.* NY: Norton, 1986.

Gerges, Fawaz A. *Journey of the Jihadist.* New York: Harcourt, 2006.

Gladwell, Malcolm. *Blink.* New York: Little Brown, 2005.

Greenwald, David S., and Steven J. Zeitlin. *No Reason to Talk About It: Families Confront the Nuclear Taboo.* New York: W.W. Norton and Co., 1987.

Hardy, Kenneth V. and Tracey A. Laszloffy. *Teens Who Hurt: Clinical Interventions to Break the Cycle of Adolescent Violence.* New York: Guilford Press, 2005.

Horgan, John. *The Psychology of Terrorism.* New York: Routledge, 2005.

Human Rights Watch. *Recurring Nightmares: State Responsibility for "Disappearances" and "Abductions" in Sri Lanka.* New York: Human Rights Watch, 2008.

Jaganathan, Pradeep. *At the Water's Edge.* New York: South Focus Press, 2004.

Jones, Marie. *A November Night and Stones in His Pockets.* London: Nick Hern Books, 2000.

Kagitcibasi, Cigdem. "The Autonomous, Relational Self: A New Synthesis." *European Psychologist* 1, no. 3 (1996): 180–6.

Kean, Thomas. Transcript from Meet The Press, May 29, 2005. Retrieved from www.msnbc.com on July 22, 2004.

Keairns, Yvonne E. "The Voices of Girl Child Soldiers: Sri Lanka." In *The Voices of Girl Child Soldiers,* no. 66. New York, NY: Quaker United Nations Office, 2003.

Kegan, Robert. *The Evolving Self: Problem and Process in Human Development.* Cambridge, MA: Harvard University Press, 1982.

———. *In Over Our Heads: The Mental Demands of Modern Life.* Cambridge, MA: Harvard University Press, 1994.

Kimmel, Paul R., and Chris E. Stout. *Collateral Damage.* Edited by Chris E. Stout. Westport, CT: Praeger, 2006.

Kliman, Jodie, ed. *Touched by War Zones, Near and Far: Oscillations of Despair and Hope.* Edited by Betty Mae Kune-Karrer. Vol. 1, no. 1. AFTA Monograph Series. Washington, DC: American Family Therapy Association, 2005.

Kohlberg, Lawrence. *The Philosophy of Moral Development: Moral Stages and the Idea of Justice.* New York: Harper and Row, 1981.

Kozol, Jonathon. *Savage Inequalities: Children in America's Schools.* New York: Harper Perennial, 1992.

Krueger, Alan, and Maleckova, Jitka. "Education, Poverty, and Terrorism: Is There a Causal Connection?" *Journal of Economic Perspectives* 17, no. 4 (2003): 119–144.

Kruglanski, Arie W., and Shira Fishman. "Terroism Between 'Syndrome' and 'Tool'." *Current Directions in Psychological Science* 15, no. 1 (2006): 45–48.

LoCicero, Alice, and Samuel Justin Sinclair, "Terrorism and Terrorist Leaders: Insights from Developmental and Ecological Psychology." *Studies in Conflict and Terrorism* 31, no. 3 (2008): 227–50.

Malraux, Andre. *Man's Fate*. New York: Modern Library, 1934.

McCauley, Clark. "Psychological Issues in Understanding Terrorism and the Response to Terrorism." In *Psychology of Terrorism,* edited by Chris E. Stout, 33–66. Westport, CT; Praeger, 2004.

McCauley, Clark. "Psychological Issues in Understanding Terrorism and the Response to Terrorism." In *Collateral Damage: The Psychological Consequences of America's War on Terrorism,* edited by Chris E. Stout. Westport, CT: Praeger Security International, 2006.

Merari, Ariel. "Psychological Aspects of Suicide Terrorism." In *Psychology of Terrorism.* edited by Bruce Bongar, Lisa M. Brown, Larry E. Beutler, James N. Breckenridge, and Philip G. Zimbardo, 101–15. New York: Oxford University Press, 2007.

Mitchell, James A. "Soldier Girl?" *Humanist* 66, no. 5 (2006): 5.

Moghaddam, Assaf. *The Roots of Terrorism.* New York: Chelsea House, 2006.

Moghaddam, Fathali. *From the Terrorists' Point of View.* Westport, CT: Praeger Security International, 2006.

Narosky, Jose. *Aforismos De Oro/Gold Aphorisms.* Buenos Aires: El Ateneo, 2005.

Nathan, Otto, and Heinz Norden. *Einstein on Peace.* New York: Simon and Schuster, 1960.

Paley, Vivian. *Bad Guys Don't Have Birthdays: Fantasy Play at Four.* Chicago: University of Chicago Press, 1991.

Patchett, Ann. *Bel Canto.* New York, NY: Harpercollins, 2002.

Piaget, Jean. *The Construction of Reality in the Child.* Oxford, England: Basic Books, 1954.

Pilisuk, Mark, and Jenifer Achord Rountree. *Who Benefits from Global Violence and War: Uncovering a Destructive System, Contemporary Psychology.* Westport, CT: Praeger Security International, 2008.

Rabain-Jamin, Jacqueline. "Language Socialization of the Child in African Families Living in France." In *Cross Cultural Roots of Minority Child Development,* edited by Patricia M. Greenfield and Rodney R. Cocking, 147–166. Hillsdale, NJ: Lawrence Erlaum, 1994.

Rogoff, Barbara, Jayanthi Mistry, Artin Goncu, and Chirstine Mosier. "Guided Participation in Cultural Activity by Toddlers and Caregivers." *Monographs of the Society for Research in Child Development* 58, no. 8 (1993): 1–174.

Rosen, David M. *Armies of the Young: Child Soldiers in War and Terrorism.* New Brunswick, NJ: Rutgers University Press, 2005.

Scheuer, Michael. *Imperial Hubris.* Washington, DC: Brassey's, Inc, 2004.

Seligman, Martin E. *Learned Optimism: How to Change Your Mind and Your Life.* New York: Vintage, 2006.

Selman, Robert L. *The Promotion of Social Awareness: Powerful Lessons from the Partnership of Developmental Theory and Classroom Practice.* New York: Russell Sage Foundation, 2007.

Shipler, David. *Arabs and Jews: Wounded Spirits in the Promised Land,* paperback edition, New York: Penguin Press, 2002.

Soans, Robin. *Talking to Terrorists.* London: Oberon Books, 2006.

Stern, Jessica. *Terror in the Name of God.* New York: Harpercollins, 2003.

"The Terrorism Index." *Foreign Policy,* July/August 2006, http://web1 .foreignpolicy.com/issue_julyaug_2006/TI-index/index.html.

Updike, John. *Terrorist.* NY: Ballantine Books, 2006.

Wessells, Michael. *Child Soldiers: From Violence to Protection.* Cambridge, MA: Harvard University Press, 2006.

Wessels, Michael. "A Living Wage." In *A World Turned Upside Down,* edited by Neil Boothby, Allison Strang, and Michael Wessels, 179–98. Bloomfield, CT: Kumarian Press, 2006.

White, Ralph. "Misperception and War." *Peace and Conflict* 10, no. 4 (2004): 399–409.

Zimbardo, Philip. *The Lucifer Effect.* New York: Random House, 2007.

INDEX

adolescent: as character in fiction, 19; cognitive development and reasoning in, 8, 20–21, 33, 39, 47; collectivism and, 35; development of, 59; emotions of, 21; interview responses of, 51; recruitment of, 32; and respect, importance of, 105; and risk, approach to, 57; and social groups, importance of, 49

Afghanistan: child soldiers in, 83; training camp in, 90; war in, 84

Ahmad, character in *Terrorist,* 19–21, 102

Allison, Graham, 88–89

altruism, 23–24, 35, 75

American: children, 59, 86, 97; children, similarity with Sri Lankans, 2, 51, 53; collaboration, 94–96; Gold Star mothers, 72; media, 26, 77, 98; soldiers, 73–74; soldiers' families and friends, 84; terrorist, in fiction, 19; veterans, 72; views of terrorism and terrorists, 13, 17, 21, 22, 26–27, 31, 32, 54, 58, 74, 76–77, 84, 99–100

American Family Therapy Association (AFTA): monograph on effects of war, 96, 117

Americans: and al Qaeda, 89; distribution of wealth, 27; ignoring other areas of the world, 6, 53, 77, 78, 83; knowledge of child soldiers, 21; lack of knowledge of war, 53; others views of, 17, 83, 100; threat of nuclear war and, 86, 89; ties with others, 6; ways to work toward peace, 8, 91

Amnesty International, report of child soldiers, 33

Angola, child soldiers in, 83

anti-American, 21

Arnestad, Beate, 16, 115

Atran, Scott, 49, 115

bad guys: imaginary, in children's play, 97–100, 107; oppressors seen as bad guys, 104; term used by press, public officials, 97–100, 109; terrorists not seen as bad guys, 107

Bad Guys Don't Have Birthdays, 97, 116

Bel Canto, 13, 19, 37, 117

black tigers, 21, 79

Blair, Tony, Former British Prime Minister, 108

Boucher, Richard (Assistant Secretary of State), 99

brain: development of, 33–34; youthful, 41, 115

Bronfenbrenner, Urie, 8, 42, 49, 78, 115
Bush, George W., President, 88, 99, 107

Cameroon, child soldiers in, 83
Canada, Geoffrey, 43–44, 116
Carmen, character in *Bel Canto,* 13, 19, 20–21, 37, 102
Challenger spacecraft disaster, 39–40
Chance for Peace Address, 101
child soldier: coercion of, 21, 74, 103–4; defined, 57; fictional, 20; former, 18; international conditions and, 79; risks associated with being, 20; in Sri Lanka, 58, 83, 113; sources of knowledge about, 22, 58; similarities to child terrorist, 17, 27, 32; similarities to government-sponsored soldiers, 73–74, 104; social science and, 18, 70; in various countries, 32–33, 36, 83, 101, 115; voluntary, 3, 43, 59, 73, 99; United Nations and, 84
child terrorist, 18–19, 21–22, 26–27, 32, 74, 77, 79, 82, 85, 104
civilian: costs of war to, 71, 73, 86; perceived as enemies in war, 46, 73; as victims of war, 2, 4, 24, 71, 73, 86; as victims of Iraq war, 112; as victims of nuclear war, 54, 86; as victims of terrorism, 2, 4, 16, 24, 71; as terrorist targets, 12, 16, 24, 32, 74, 77
cognitive, 34, 40, 49, 77, 98
cognitive development, 8, 33–35, 45, 47
collective deprivation, 45
collective experiences, 72
collective identity, 35, 45
collective thought, 36
collective values, 37, 47
collectivist cultures, 53, 92, 112
Colombia, child soldiers in, 16, 83
Council on Foreign Relations, 108

Daae, Morton, 21, 115
development, 35, 42, 45; of adolescent, 33, 41, 59; biological, 43; of brain, 33–34; of child, 33–34, 59, 117, 118; of child soldiers, 59, 70; cognitive, 8, 33–35, 45,

47; domain specificity of, 39; emotional, 33–34; moral, 36; physical, 33; positive, 8, 46; psychosocial, 40; social, 8, 33; stages of, 116–17; technological, 54; of youth, 8
developmental, 46–48
developmental limitations, 20
developmental psychologists, 85
developmental psychology, 59
developmental science, 33
developmental vulnerability, 49
developmentally oriented education, 46
domain, cognitive, 39, 40, 44

ecological, 7, 42, 44, 78, 117
ecology, 42
Economist, The, 98, 107, 113
education, 7, 20, 26, 39, 46, 56, 74, 77, 82, 102, 104, 105, 111; and terrorism, 117
educational institutions, 81
educational materials, 112
educational opportunity, 104
educational system, 8
Einstein, Albert, 86, 88, 115, 117
Eisenhower, Dwight D., 101
emotional development, 33–34
Erikson, Erik, 18, 40, 48, 116
ethnic conflict, 22, 51, 55–56, 59, 92–94, 104, 108
ethnic group, 37, 41, 52–53, 60, 74, 82, 92–93, 96, 98
ethnic violence, 22, 51, 55–56, 59, 92–94, 104, 108
ethnic war, 22, 51, 55–56, 59, 92–94, 104, 108
ethnicity, 39, 92–93, 96
ethnic tamil, 20, 105

Fishman, Shira, 48, 117
friends (Quakers), 96

gangs, 42, 29, 50
gist thinking, 10, 15–16, 41–42, 45
Gold Star Mothers, 72, 112
Good Friday Agreement, 108
Greenwald, David, 54, 55, 116

hearts and minds, 72–73, 101–2, 104–7, 109
human rights: advocates for, 6; U.S. denial of aid due to violations of, 2; United States as potential advocate for, 106, 107, 109; violations of, 77, 80, 82, 83, 96, 107; violations of, connected to terrorism, 82, 103; violations of, in Sri Lanka, 2, 78, 82, 105, 113
Human Rights Watch, 2, 111

identity: group, 25–26, 34–35, 37, 41, 45, 47–50, 81–82, 91–93; personal, 25, 35, 40, 48, 92; political, 40; religious, 40
immigrant, 81–82, 104
India, child soldiers in, 83
individual: focus of psychology, 35; identity of, 35, 45; oriented to culture, 35–37, 40–41, 80, 112
Indonesia, child soldiers in, 83
International Herald Tribune, using term "bad guys," 98, 99, 107, 113
Islam: extremist interpretation of, 15; Osama bin Laden and, 89; religion of, 32, 77
Islamic jihadist, 19, 77
Islamic terrorism, 17, 21, 45
Islamist, 17

Jaganathan, Pradeep, 105, 116
Jones, Marie, 100, 116

Keairns, Yvonne E., 18, 23, 116
Kegan, Robert, 41, 49, 116
Khan, Dr. Abdul Qadeer, 89
Krueger, Alan, 105, 117
Kruglanski, Arie, 48, 117

legal infrastructure, 75, 80–81
London, terrorist attacks in, 15–16, 37, 100
LTTE, 2, 3, 6, 52, 58, 69. See also Tamil Tigers; accusations of kidnapping, 2, 58; Black Tigers, 21; condemned by other countries, 2; end of ceasefire with Sri Lankan government, 52

Madrid: terrorism conference in, 9, 11; terrorist attacks in, 15–16, 48, 100
Maleckova, Jitka, 105, 117
martyrdom, as motivation for terrorism, by gender, 25–26
martyrs: terrorists viewed as, 16, 41, 46–48; terrorist viewing self as, 7, 24, 32, 72, 79; Sri Lanka and terrorist viewed as, 3
Maslow, Abraham H., and hierarchy of needs, 102–3
Meichenbaum, Donald, 102
Merari, Ariel, 32, 47–50, 117
Mitchell, Senator George, 108
McCauley, Clark, 14, 24, 37, 117
Moghaddam, Fathali, 44–47, 75, 107, 117
My Daughter the Terrorist, 21, 79, 112

Nepal, child soldiers in, 83
Northern Ireland, 7, 56, 108
Norway: assistance with ceasefire in Sri Lanka, 52; Nordic monitors in Sri Lanka, 80
nuclear attack, 71, 76, 86, 88
nuclear disarmament, 87
nuclear disaster, as catastrophe, 76, 84–86
nuclear suitcase weapon, 90
nuclear terrorism, 88, 115
nuclear threat, 54–55, 85–88
nuclear weapons, 10–11, 54, 76, 83–85, 87–89

Osama bin Laden: and Afghanistan training camps, 89; and CIA unit, 89; and Islamic community, 89; as prototype terrorist, 17; preparing for future attack, 89; seeking nuclear weapon, 88;

Padilla, Jose, 99
Palestinian terrorists, 27, 48
Paley, Vivian, 97, 100, 107, 117
Patchett, Ann, 19, 102, 107, 117
Pilisuk, Marc, 97, 117
Post, Jerrold, 15
Public Conversations Project, 96, 113
Pugwash, Nobel Prize awarded to, 88, 96

Quakers, 96, 116

Red Cross: as international relief agency, 53, 103; portrayed as intermediary in *Bel Canto,* 13; in Sri Lanka, 3; refugee camp, 58, 101, 110
Refusing to be Enemies, film of Zeitouna group, 96, 113
Rosen, David, 43, 53, 57, 118
Rwanda, child soldiers in, 83

sarvodaya, 96
Scheuer, Michael, 89, 113, 118
September 11, 2001 (9/11): attackers as prototypes, 16–17; attacks on the United States on, 11; bin Laden and, 89; increased interest in terrorism after, 14, 78, 89; psychology of attackers, 25, 107; reactions of Americans to, 28, 59, 84, 95, 108
Shipler, David, 105, 118
Sinhalese ethnicity, 6, 52–53, 55
Soans, Robin, 21, 107, 118
social development, 8, 33
society of friends, 96
Soldiers, child. *See* child soldier
Sri Lanka: American lack of knowledge about, 78; awareness of nuclear weapons in, 83; child soldiers in, 3, 22–23, 57, 59, 79, 83; civil war in, 3, 51–52; civilians of, affected by war, 4, 51, 53; collectivist values and, 34–36, 53, 87, 92; government of, ending ceasefire, 52; human rights violations in, 2, 6, 78, 80, 82, 105, 113, 111; lack of objective news accounts about, 80; literacy rates in, 79; people of, 3; suicide/martyr attacks in, 3; terrorism in, 6; tsunami of 2004 in, 2–3, 5, 52, 82, 85–86, 92; U.S. military aid to, 2, 82
Sudan, child soldiers in, 83

Talking to Terrorists, play by Robin Soans, 21, 118
Tamil, ethnicity, 1, 3, 6, 51–53, 55–56, 105
Tamil Tigers (Liberation Tigers of Tamil Eelam), 2, 52, 105, 111. *See also* LTTE
terrorism, 8–29; difficulty defining, 17; conditions that foster, 6–7, 78; frequency of, worldwide, 32; and grievances of terrorist organizations, 24; government-sponsored, 24; prevention of, 25, 72–73, 106–7; war on, 101
terrorist: aspects of development of, 40, 45; child, difficulty defining, 17, 19, 22. *See* child terrorist; family members of, 72, 74, 76; motivation of, 3, 19, 21–23, 25–26, 44, 59, 78; nuclear, 88–92; organizations, 18, 37, 45, 47, 49, 89, 103–4; reactions to, 28–29, 31, 71, 77, 86; research about, 7–8, 8–29, 54, 83, 104, 112
tsunami of 2004, in Sri Lanka, 2–3, 5, 52, 82, 85–86, 92

Uganda, child soldiers in, 83
UNICEF, 53, 103
United Nations: and aid, 5; and child soldiers, 57, 58, 84–85; and human rights, 106, 113; and nuclear weapons, 86; and terrorism, 12, 14
Updike, John, author of *Terrorist,* 19, 21, 102, 118

Wessells, Michael, and child soldiers, 33, 53, 57, 103, 111, 118
Women's Action for Nuclear Disarmament, 87

Zeitlin, Steven, 54–55, 85, 116
Zeitouna, 113
Zimbardo, Philip, 25, 118

About the Series

The Praeger Series in Contemporary Psychology

In this series, experts from various disciplines peer through the lens of psychology telling us answers they see for questions of human behavior. Their topics may range from humanity's psychological ills—addictions, abuse, suicide, murder and terrorism among them—to works focused on positive subjects including intelligence, creativity, athleticism and resilience. Regardless of the topic, the goal of this series remains constant—to offer innovative ideas, provocative considerations and useful beginnings to better understand human behavior.

Series Editor

Chris E. Stout, PsyD, MBA
Founding Director, Center for Global Initiatives
Clinical Professor, College of Medicine, University of Illinois at Chicago

Advisory Board

Bruce E. Bonecutter, PhD
University of Illinois at Chicago
Director, Behavioral Services, Elgin Community Mental Health Center

Joseph A. Flaherty, MD
University of Illinois College of Medicine and College of Public Health
Chief of Psychiatry, University of Illinois Hospital

Michael Horowitz, PhD
Chicago School of Professional Psychology
President, Chicago School of Professional Psychology

Sheldon I. Miller, MD
Northwestern University
Director, Stone Institute of Psychiatry, Northwestern Memorial Hospital

Dennis P. Morrison, PhD
Chief Executive Officer, Center for Behavioral Health, Indiana
President, Board of Directors, Community Healthcare Foundation, Indiana

William H. Reid, MD
University of Texas Health Sciences Center
Chair, Scientific Advisory Board, Texas Depressive and Manic Depressive Association

Recent Titles in Contemporary Psychology

Psychology of Terrorism, Condensed Edition: Coping with the Continuing Threat
Chris E. Stout, editor

Handbook of International Disaster Psychology, Volumes I–IV
Gilbert Reyes and Gerard A. Jacobs, editors

The Psychology of Resolving Global Conflicts: From War to Peace, Volumes 1-3
Mari Fitzduff and Chris E. Stout, editors

The Myth of Depression as Disease: Limitations and Alternatives to Drug Treatment
Allan M. Leventhal and Christopher R. Martell

Preventing Teen Violence: A Guide for Parents and Professionals
Sherri N. McCarthy and Claudio Simon Hutz

Making Enemies Unwittingly: Humiliation and International Conflict
Evelin Gerda Lindner

Collateral Damage: The Psychological Consequences of America's War on Terrorism
Paul R. Kimmel and Chris E. Stout, editors

Terror in the Promised Land: Inside the Anguish of the Israeli-Palestinian Conflict
Judy Kuriansky, editor

Trauma Psychology, Volumes 1 and 2
Elizabeth Carll, editor

Beyond Bullets and Bombs: Grassroots Peace Building between Israelis and Palestinians
Judy Kuriansky, editor

Who Benefits from Global Violence and War: Uncovering a Destructive System
Marc Pilisuk with Jennifer Rountree

Right Brain/Left Brain Leadership: Shifting Style for Maximum Impact
Mary Lou Décosterd

ABOUT THE AUTHORS

Dr. Alice LoCicero is Past President of the Society for Terrorism Research. A board certified Clinical Psychologist and a Massachusetts Behavioral Health Disaster Responder, her specialty is working with adolescents and young adults, especially around issues of oppression, trauma, and loss. Formerly a faculty member at the Center for Multicultural Training in Psychology at Boston Medical Center, and founding Director of a service reflecting a partnership between Suffolk University and the Massachusetts Juvenile Court to provide counseling to court-involved youth, Dr. LoCicero is currently Associate Professor and Chair of Social Science at Endicott College, where she is a member of the Advisory Board for the Center on Workplace and School Violence. She traveled to Sri Lanka in May and June of 2007 to study firsthand the conditions that make terrorism an appealing idea to some youth. In earlier parts of her career, Dr. LoCicero was a Staff Psychologist at Children's Hospital, Boston, a Clinical Instructor at Harvard Medical School, and a contributing author to the popular women's health reference guide *Our Bodies, Ourselves.*

Dr. Samuel Justin Sinclair is cofounder and President of the Society for Terrorism Research (STR; www.societyforterrorismresearch.org), and is currently a Fellow in Psychology at the Massachusetts General Hospital and Harvard Medical School. In addition, he is cofounder and coeditor-in-chief of the peer-refereed journal, Terrorism Research, and has developed and collaborated with an international Editorial Board comprised of roughly eighty experts representing fourteen countries and five continents. He has published numerous papers in the areas of terrorism, aggression, violence, psychological assessment, and

psychometrics, and continues to have active research programs in these areas. Dr. Sinclair is also the developer of the Terrorism Catastrophizing Scale (TCS), a new psychological assessment tool measuring anticipatory fears about terrorism. He is past recipient of the Association for Threat Assessment Professional's (ATAP) Dr. Chris Hatcher Memorial Scholarship Award (2007), and his research and scholarship has been featured in numerous publications. Dr. Sinclair's clinical and research interests are in terrorism, aggression, violence, risk assessment, psychological and neuropsychological assessment, psychometrics, and forensic psychology.